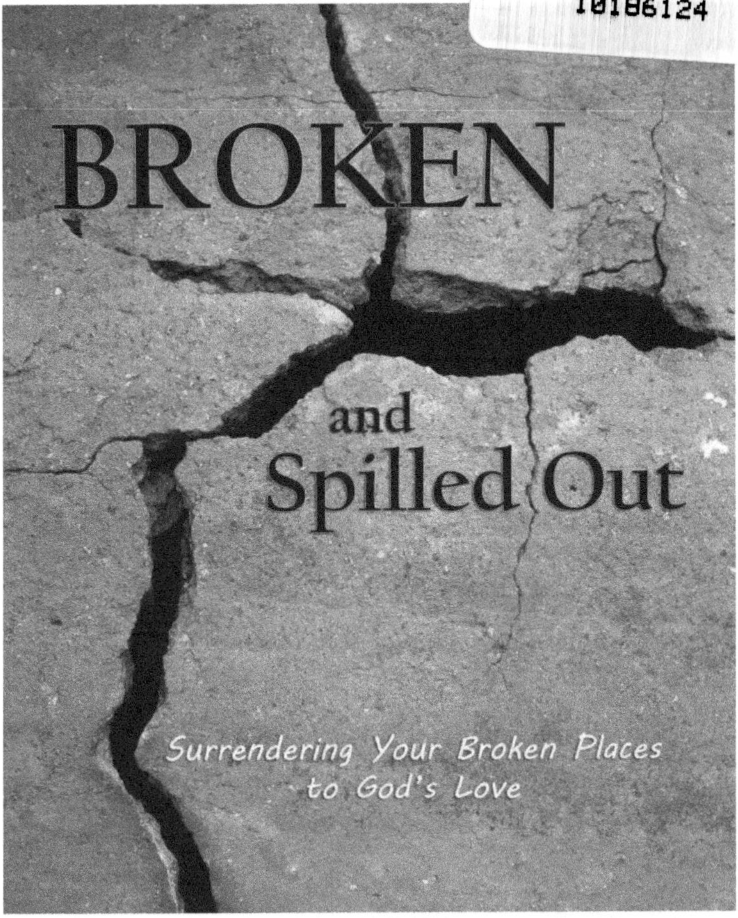
BROKEN
and
Spilled Out
Surrendering Your Broken Places
to God's Love

By Carol Hogan

Creative Force Press

Broken and Spilled Out
© 2017 by Carol Hogan
www.CarolHogan.com

This title is also available as an eBook. Visit www.CreativeForcePress.com/titles for more information.

Published by Creative Force Press
4704 Pacific Ave, Suite C, Lacey, WA 98503
www.CreativeForcePress.com

All rights reserved. No part of this publication may be reproduced, stored in a retrieval system, or transmitted in any form or by any means--for example, electronic, photocopy, recording--without the prior written permission of the publisher.

ISBN: 978-1-939989-28-4

Printed in the United States of America

*Find hope and trust in your Heavenly Father.
He is waiting patiently for you to call out to Him today.*

This is a courageous work. Thank you, Carol, for your courage to live it, and to RE live it, that others might be free through the pursuing love of the Father. My prayer is that your story inspires, emboldens and equips others to invite their Abba Father to lead them on their own journey toward the healing, restoration and abundant life He has prepared for them. Thank you for your honest, transparent, blow-by-blow testimony to the truth that God indeed will redeem every painful, shameful thing of our past to work *for* our glorious future in Him.

—Deborah Kristen, Program Director, The Clearing

The message is clear, there is hope for everyone! Carol Hogan's true life story brings a reality to the human condition, bringing to light an even greater reality: God has a plan for all those who are in Him. The raw, unfiltered delivery of her story captures the reader and keeps them coming for more.

—Mingo Barron, Youth Pastor, Christian City Fellowship

Carol takes us on a transparent journey of her life that is both honest and raw as she vividly describes how she got into her self-made *pit*. But the story doesn't end there! The latter half of her book beautifully depicts how God lovingly embraced her in the mess and pulled her out of the pit into freedom in Christ. This book is a must read for all who are ready to exchange their pit for His freedom!

—Kelly Turner, Counselor, M.Ed., LPC-I

TABLE OF CONTENTS

Introduction: Assignment from God 7

Chapter 1: Building a Customized Pit 10

Chapter 2: My First Steps Into Freedom 39

Chapter 3: Journey on the Mountain 58

Chapter 4: Freedom Walk 76

Chapter 5: The Healing Continues 87

Chapter 6: The Teaching Continues 96

Chapter 7: Freedom Reigns! 105

Starting Your Own Journey with God 117

Resources 120

Acknowledgments 121

About the Author 125

Introduction

Assignment from God

All of us have a life story. This is mine. You will read about my customized pit, my brokenness, healing, and finally, my restoration. I will share with you some of my journal entries from 55 journals I have kept over the last 21 years. I have asked the Lord, my God, if my life was to be an open book like King David's. His answer to me was "Yes." "Okay, *Lord, but what do You want me to say about my story? How do I sort out what needs to be written, what needs to be put aside, what wounds need to be healed?*"

True to His Word, He said, "Trust me, child. I will help you. Just bring yourself to the throne room. I will help you. It's like sorting out the pieces to a puzzle, and only I know what the final picture looks like. You will have to trust Me to guide your hand and heart as we sort." He also said, "You must journal. Others will read and identify with what you say. Others will seek Me through it. I've given you this assignment, now use it for Me."

As if that wasn't enough, He later told me that He had left me here on this earth for 70 years *because He trusted me.* When He revealed this, it was like a cattle prod sending shock waves throughout my body. I quivered and still quiver when I repeat it. All the pain, all the suffering, all the loneliness, all the everything...*You trusted me to endure.* "You trust me for what?" I asked, and He said, "For others." With that answer, how could I refuse Him?

So here am I, putting the pieces of my life before you.

Lord, reveal to me those things easily remembered and those I've hidden so deep that they don't come to mind. Bring all that You desire to the surface. I know the pieces are shaped by my feelings. I know the feelings are associated with my needs. I trust You to help me identify what true needs the feelings represent. I take all of the needs to the Cross and be healed. I am taking Your hand like a child and revisiting my pit. I am trusting you to bring me safely back out. I used to see Your light above me, I now see your light was with me in my low, dark pit. I was not alone. I can trust You. You ask me to take one step at a time...just one. Here is my first step back into a darkness that once ruled my life. Cover me with Your wings.

Deep breath, Carol. Take a deep breath and trust this is all for His glory. Others need to see, read and hear how He is transforming me. They need to know the depth of the transformation, and will only know it if I bring the *yuck* out in the open. No more secret places. Be transparent.

Being transparent and bringing the yuck out in the open requires you to read highlights (or should I say, lowlights) of what made up my customized pit. I want you to understand the depth of my wounds, which I'll expose in Chapter 1. My healing process begins in Chapter 2. From

Chapter 3 on, you will begin to see God's conversations with me as I began stepping into my freedom.

Yes, freedom! Freedom is available to *all* regardless of how wounded we may be. He loved me enough to pursue me. He loves you enough, too. He is pursuing you. Let Him catch you. Your journey towards healing and freedom are within your grasp.

Chapter 1

Building a Customized Pit

"... you brought me up from the pit, O Lord my God. Yes, He brought me out of my pit...with His love He brought me out."
Jonah 2:6

There are several HUGE words in my life, and the first one is *Trust*. To have transparency implies trust, and trust is a big word...no, a HUGE word. I thought I had successfully deleted it from my vocabulary many years ago.

You see, I learned as a child not to trust anyone, not family, not friends, and later in life, not even my co-workers. Trusting equaled hurt and pain, and I wasn't going to allow *anyone* to hurt me if I could help it. Many of you know exactly what I mean. Did you know that a child should be able to trust their father, their mother, their sisters and their brothers? I only understood that truth when I was in my 40's and fighting for my life as I spiraled down into a serious clinical depression. But, I'm getting ahead of myself. Let's go back to the beginning and put the border pieces on this puzzle.

All stories have a beginning, middle and end. So does this one. What I didn't realize was that my beginning included building a customized pit at a very young age. Who in their right mind decides to build a customized pit and stays there for 58 years? The answer? No one. No one builds, steps into and stays in a pit on purpose. I say it was *customized*, because it fit my circumstances, past experiences, personality and outlook. It was a pit just for me.

Pits are tricky. Many don't even recognize they're in one. I built a pit, although others have built walls around themselves. Whether it's a pit or walls, they are constructed out of pain in an unsuccessful attempt to shield ourselves from *more* pain. And, either way, what we build isolates and keeps us from being the free child God created us to be.

But let's get back to what I built…a pit…a customized pit. Since God asked me to describe my pit, I thought I'd better look up the definition and then see how my life mirrored it. Well, Webster's Dictionary defines a pit as "a hole or cavity in the ground, an abyss." An abyss…yep, that describes it *perfectly*. But, what did my abyss look like from the inside? It had a hollow center. At least at the time I felt like *I* had a hollow center. Everything seemed to be on the surface: feelings, attitudes, emotions. I had become an emotional ticking time bomb.

In one sense, the high vertical walls of my pit/abyss were really a protection for those around me. I rarely exploded, because to explode showed weakness and vulnerability.

Those emotions were deadly to my survival. *I must not appear to be weak in any area...that would surely be used against me.* But, what made up those high vertical walls of my pit? The answer was painful, when God revealed it. He said "Deep Rejection." Really...deep rejection? I would have thought it would have been loneliness. Ah-ha...new revelation: loneliness often comes from deep rejection. But trusting God, I began looking at my life to see where the rejection started.

All beginnings have a birth, and I was born into a family that consisted of my mother, father, one sister and three brothers. Dysfunctional is a word that became popular several years ago and it surely described my family. I grew up in this family basically alone. Two of my brothers and my sister were older, and had neither the time nor the desire to be with me. That is, until it was night time. I learned to dread darkness, and even to this day I have trouble sleeping at night. Can you imagine the anger I felt when later in life I would often hear the statement, "The Bells are just oversexed." *What do you mean oversexed?* The truth is they never learned any boundaries from my father, who was deep into pornography. They never learned to respect females...

A well-known Christian leader said it well, "An emotional bombshell hit our home...and lives continued to be torn by the shrapnel no one ever swept away." My family was hit and wounded by shrapnel that no one wanted to clean up. It resulted in alcoholics and sex addicts. On November 2, 2011, I wrote down the scripture verse Luke 23:34. "Jesus said, Father, forgive them for they do not know what they are doing…'"

Please understand, I have forgiven them. But, do I still need to forgive them at a deeper level? I'm waiting for God to show me the answer to that question. I believe He is slowly revealing it, because I had also written, "Lord, my family didn't know they were killing my childhood and most of my adulthood…they didn't know. But *You* knew God. You knew the depth of the death I was experiencing. You are restoring what was lost.

In another one of my journals I had written, "You have wept with me. You have wept for the wrong done to me. You have wept for all that was taken. You wept with me in my aloneness." Yes, He will restore that which was unjustly taken. He will replace double. What an incredible promise to look forward to, as restoration continues to come in my life. I believe a greater depth of forgiveness for my family is still coming. *God, I believe You will restore all that was lost.*

The surface is where I lived during my youth. It was a surface created by the hundreds of books I read. When I discovered the library, I discovered a goldmine. I could check out eight books at a time read them all in a week and go back for more. Books gave me an escape into another world. This world was made up of romance, adventure and intrigue. You name it, it was there for me to absorb. But, this world was not real.

As a young girl of ten, I walked into an unfamiliar church by myself and went to Sunday school class. No parent's hand to hold, no encouragement…just me walking to a church by myself and going into a class, where I didn't know anyone. Can you imagine that? I look back on this time *now* and see the protective arms of my Heavenly Father surrounding me and holding me close. He wanted me to be in a safe place, hearing about Him.

He continued to shield me all the way through high school, as I stayed involved with a church youth group. His shield kept me from *getting into trouble*, but it didn't keep me from being an overachiever. I can remember thinking to myself, *if I am better than most, maybe I will be loved and accepted.* I felt desperately insignificant, only I didn't know it, and that feeling lasted for decades.

But, back to my high school days.

High school consisted of football games, after game parties at the church, getting A's and working. I started working at age 16 in the local library. How perfect! It was here I made one dollar an hour, and with the money I was able to get my first pair of glasses, my yearbooks and my clothes. My parents didn't provide these basics, and I was learning at a young age to take care of myself. I was still learning not to trust anyone or anything, only myself, and mistrust became the foundation upon which I built my life. The walls of the customized pit I was (unknowingly) building consisted of mistrust. As the next season of my life unfolded, I continued to take care of myself, by myself. I moved away from home and took a job in a paint manufacturing plant. But, I also moved away from the protection of my church family and fell further into my pit, hitting an incredibly rough bottom.

Rough does not even begin to describe the first major event and its impact on my life. I kept it buried so deep; so deep that it was a secret for 33 years.

On August 3, 1999 I wrote the following as part one of a three-part assignment given to me by a therapist. Just to warn you, it is intense. I still feel the emotions to this day, but now I grieve for the young girl, me, who just wanted to be loved and to love in return.

> Today begins a painful journey into the past; painful because it will bring forth events, conversations and actions that I have not really dealt with until this time of my life. I pray right now, God, that You go before me and be my guide. Show me what needs to be written, show me what parts of my heart need to be healed, for indeed it has been wounded.
>
> I was 19 and living in a one-bedroom apartment in Yorba Linda, California. I was working in the research lab of Sprayon, Inc. It was here that I met Freddie. What a good-looking guy he was. Dark,

wavy hair, dark eyes and an incredible smile. We began dating, and strangely I can't remember anything that we did, except for two of our dates.

One of the dates entailed driving from Yorba Linda to Upland to see my parents on a Sunday afternoon. Freddie wasn't very happy about it, and the time spent with my parents was strained. So much for the happy event of a girl taking a boy home to meet the parents. I remember being disappointed and hurt. Thoughts of rejection sprung up once again. Back at my apartment we made love, and then Freddie got up and left. It seemed that he was always leaving and I was left behind with no one to talk to. My only means of communication was the telephone, but who would I call? My sister had her own life to live, and I didn't have a car to get around. Life was pretty confining.

The second date with Freddie occurred in September. Why I recall the month I have no idea, except that major events in my life seem to occur in September. This was to be one of the biggest "life markers" of my life, past, present and future. It began with Freddie picking me up and taking me to his house which was located next to the railroad tracks. I remember the night as being very beautiful and wondering why we had come to his home. We had never done this before.

Anyway, Freddie got out and I followed him into the house. No one else was home in the tiny, cramped place. Freddie took me immediately to a bedroom and without even taking off my clothes, had sex with me, and then got up and went to the bathroom. I laid there, feeling dirty and used, wondering why I was being treated this way and knowing that the "relationship" with Freddie was coming to an end. I also knew that I felt strangely different and wondered if I had just become pregnant. I don't even remember what transpired next. Isn't it strange, how one can block things from one's mind?

I do remember that I continued to work at Sprayon and one day realized I was pregnant. Panic set in. What was I to do? Where was I to go? Who could help me? I knew from past events, that Mom and Dad would be of no help. I was on my own. I had *made my bed, now I was to lie in it.* This was Mom's saying whenever I needed help, reassurance or encouragement. Indeed I had made my own bed. I told Freddie and his comment was to get an abortion. But he had no name to give and wouldn't help. In desperation, I called Berta (my sister), and asked her if she knew of any doctor that did abortions. Yes, I'm sad to say, I thought this was my only option. She said she would try to find one, but instead called Mom and Dad.

Imagine my shock, when I got off of work one day and went to Berta's only to find both of my parents waiting for me. Mom didn't waste any time and said that I would not, under any circumstances, have an abortion. I don't remember her offering any other solutions, like "come home with us and we'll help you through this." No. Instead, she said that Berta was working with the social work department in Tustin to get me into a home. I was to quit my job and come home until the particulars could be worked out. There were no words of encouragement, acceptance, love or caring. I was a problem that had to be dealt with...I felt like I was an inconvenience to her...an object of shame that she had to endure.

The feelings of being a shameful object were magnified when Dad drove me home. As we stopped and parked in front of my apartment building, Dad reached over and started hugging, fondling and kissing me on the mouth. I was stunned and immediately felt like I was no longer his daughter, but a slut...someone who he had no respect or love for, but saw only as a means to satisfy his sexual desires. Why, Daddy, why? Why couldn't I turn to you for comfort? In a strained and shameful voice, I asked him to stop and he did. Nothing was to be the same again, he had crossed the line. He was no longer to be trusted, ever. I had been betrayed by my own father.

The next events I can recall were moving back home and making maternity tops. As before, Mom was of no help. She seemed to be angry at me and one night while drying dishes, she basically wanted me to account for all of the wrongs and hurts she felt my brothers and sister had "done to her." I remember telling her that I couldn't and wouldn't answer for them, but that I was sorry she had been hurt by my actions, but that I was the one hurting, not her. I was the one who would carry the scars the rest of my life, not her.

It must have been shortly after that conversation that I moved to Tustin, CA, to be a live-in babysitter for a sweet couple, Ron and Peggy. They had two boys, Bradley, age three, and Brian, six. Brian was a hyperkinetic child who was never satisfied and always in trouble. Ron refused to acknowledge that he was hyperkinetic and could be helped with medication. He firmly believed Brian was just acting out and needed a firmer hand. Poor Peggy, she was helpless to help Brian. Bradley, on the other hand, was this sweet natured young boy, full of curiosity. They were just the opposite of one another.

Babysitting them, cleaning house, fixing meals and playing with them became my full-time occupation. Whenever I had a doctor's appointment, Mom would drive down and take me to the doctor and I would pay her for time and gas. I always felt that I had inconvenienced her. These were never pleasant times. We never talked about me, but rather about life in general. My pregnancy was a taboo subject; a reality, but taboo.

Berta, who lived maybe 15 minutes away, never came to see me during the entire time I stayed with Ron and Peggy. I must have been taboo to her also...an inconvenience. It seemed like my entire family had abandoned and rejected me. That would have been a true statement, except that Ray, my younger brother, knowing how lonely I was, made a point of coming down to Tustin every Sunday and took me somewhere. One time we went to Disneyland, and I wondered if he was embarrassed to be with me. You see, people were looking at us rather strangely. Bless his heart, he said he wasn't and not to worry about what others thought. Ray made this time in my life so much brighter.

It was Ray, Ron and Peggy who showed me that life was going to be okay. It was Ron who took me to the hospital the night I went into labor. I guess Peggy called either Berta or Mom and Dad. In either case, Mom and Dad showed up at the hospital. That seemed like a long night of progressive pain, until my son was born. At the sound of his cry, I burst into sobs. My son was born. My son, whom I loved was now a part of this world. My son, whom everyone had seemed to reject before he was born was now having to face what I had been facing. How could I protect him? How could I show him how much I loved him?

All of these thoughts ran through my mind as I laid on the table and sobbed. As they wheeled me to my room, Mom leaned over and said, "Tears were the last thing I expected from you." What did she think I was, a cold-hearted machine? I don't even remember if I responded. Did it really require a response from me? Thankfully, they left and I was left alone, exhausted and sobbing.

Dawn finally came and I found myself wanting to see my son. I got up, walked to the nursery and looked at him. He was so beautiful, not red or wrinkled like the rest of the babies. Once again I began sobbing from my heart and the nurses took me back to my room. I guess my sobbing upset everyone, because the doctor was called and soon I found him sitting by my bedside. He seemed so gentle and concerned. I remember him saying that he would give me some *happy pills* that would help me through this time. I don't recall their name, but do remember them being heart-shaped and pinkish in color. They did dull the senses, dull the pain, dull the reality.

As with the pregnancy, no one came except Esther, Freddie's sister and my sister, Berta. Esther was so sweet and so concerned. I remember waking up one afternoon and finding her sitting next to me. She told me that Freddie was nowhere to be found. That didn't surprise me...responsibility was not his virtue.

Apparently, Berta was there when they brought in the adoption release papers. I don't remember. She says that I became upset and wanted to know why they had not given them to me in private. I don't remember.

I returned to Ron and Peggy's and helped out until they could get another girl. Then, I remember coming home and being relieved that Mom was in Lake Tahoe helping my brother and his wife move. I remember the agony the day the final adoption papers came and I had to sign them. By my signature on those papers, I was relinquishing all rights to my son. I was saying he was no longer mine. I was saying that someone else would have the privilege and honor of raising him. Oh, how I prayed he would know that the decision did not come lightly...that I loved him so, that I wanted him to have the best life possible...a life I couldn't give to him...that I had insisted on knowing something about his parents...that I prayed they would cherish and love this gift I was giving to them.

Ray was the only one who saw and knew of the pain

that day. The papers were signed and mailed, and my son was gone. Only the pain remained. The happy pill couldn't touch this pain, so I quit taking them. I needed to face the full force of the pain and the consequences of my actions.

Fuel was added to the pain when Mom came home. I made the decision to finish college and needed financial aid to do so. With that decision made, I received the requested financial aid papers from the college and Dad was filling them out when Mom came into the dining room. Upon finding out what Dad was doing, she grabbed the papers and said, "It is no one's G-- da-- business what we do with our money. If you want to go to college, get a job and pay your own way."

Once again I was stunned by her wrath. She went on to say, "You never asked to come home, did you?" My response was, "I didn't know I had to ask to come home." She continued by saying that she would have had to accept my son, and I remember telling her, "No, you wouldn't have. If I had known you felt so strongly about him, I would have left with him and you would never have heard from me again." At this point, Dad was telling Mom to shut up. She'd said more than enough. Ray witnessed the whole thing. Shortly thereafter, I moved out of the house and into my own apartment with a roommate. We never talked about my son again. It became a taboo subject once more.

As my life went on, I often thought of my son, wondering what kind of a man he'd become, what he was doing and did he know he was loved. I still wonder. I feel compelled to resolve these questions. I don't know if my son will come toward me, or if I am to go to him. I just know that God is preparing me to meet him. Because of him I am finally facing the sexual abuse which occurred to me. Because of him I am willing to face the memories which bring only pain, shame and contempt.

I want so much to be the whole child that God created me to be…the free child with hopes and dreams…a child who can love and be loved for who she is, not what she can do…a child who can be used by God to help others make the same painful journey…to stand beside them…to stand in the gap for them when they need it. I want so much to see my son and let him know that he was not rejected by me, but was loved so much that I gave him up as a gift of love to waiting arms. I pray that he has been loved as I wanted him to be loved.

Okay, it's time to take a deep breath…a deep, deep breath and refocus. This event did indeed become the solidifying factor of my pit. Actually, I think it made up the foundation for the bottom of the pit. Because it was the foundation, it needed a name. God revealed its name...*rejection*. Rejection and/or the fear of it were to be the driving forces in my life.

I gave rejection and fear way, way too much power over me. Not only was rejection the foundation of my pit, it also became the mortar that held the other stones of the wall in place. Remember, I didn't realize I was building a customized pit. My focus was survival...day to day survival. And because I was focused on survival, I looked at my life after the loss of my son and decided to go forward with my Plan A...going to college. However, this time, I went to a junior college. I didn't ask anyone, parents, friends or the college to help. *Go to the classes, do the homework, get the grade, get the degree, and get on with life.* Moving forward was the objective. Move forward and survive.

During this moving-forward phase, I met and ended up marrying an incredible man named Pat. Pat and I were both looking for love and acceptance. He looked for it in a bottle of beer and a cue stick. I was still looking for love in my work performance. Maybe if I became the perfect wife he would let go of his beer and cue stick. Maybe if I met all of his needs, he would meet all of mine.

We both entered into our marriage with heaping piles of emotional baggage. We didn't have God at the center of our relationship, much less the standards in His Word. Worse yet, Pat didn't believe in God *at all*. I remember feeling very sad for him, but didn't know how to help him. At least I believed in God, but that was the extent of my belief. The two of us were doomed to fail, and after five years we went our separate ways…still friends, but not husband and wife.

As with my son, I went through my divorce by myself. I bought the set of divorce papers for $25, filled them out and filed for my divorce. I sat alone in the courtroom and heard the judge urge me to take at least one dollar of alimony. I refused. I watched the expressions and heard the gasps and comments of the divorce attorneys who were sitting in the front row pews waiting to represent their clients. They were stunned, especially when I stated I wanted to take out of our marriage what I had brought into it…my living room furniture and my bed, my clothes, etc. There were no children involved so no child support issues. The judge shook his head, asked me if I was sure and then granted the divorce. A chapter in my life was over. Once again I was alone and would find a way to take care of myself. Another stone had been placed on the wall of my pit. *Move Forward* became my new mantra.

So, move forward I did as I gathered up all of my legal papers and returned to my hospital job where no one even knew I was divorcing my husband. It was on that same day the Chief Financial Officer (CFO) asked me into his office and told me I wasn't performing to company standards. I was really confused because just days before I had gotten an evaluation that said I was exceeding the standards. After pointing that out to him, he still determined I hadn't been doing my job and let me go. Now I was divorced *and* unemployed. Another rejection stone was added.

I was now rejected, alone, devalued and insignificant. Those stones were making my pit darker and darker. Let me stop here and say that about a year after being fired, I was visiting the same hospital and the CFO asked me into his office. I followed him and took a seat. I was stunned when he apologized to me because he had let me go on what he later found out were lies. Whoa. Now there was a man with integrity. I was able to tell him, that had I not been let go, I would not have had the better opportunities afforded to me in my new position in San Diego.

Can you see my Heavenly Father working to get me back on track with His plan? Even when I didn't know it, He was working out the details to ensure I didn't miss what He had for me. Only new eyes and new knowledge have allowed me to look back and see His constant presence in my life. I was wandering to the left and right, and didn't hear His voice behind me saying, "This is the way... follow me." No, I was doing my own thing, my own way, but He was still there with His constant love, His constant care, His constant protection.

Unbeknownst to me, I was to need all three as I moved to San Diego and started a new chapter in my life. It was here where I gained invaluable experience and more knowledge as I helped open a brand new hospital. It was also here that I meet D.J. who was to become my soulmate friend. You know, the kind of friend that the instant you meet, you feel like you've known them your entire life. We shared clothes, ideas, took cooking classes together and covered for one another. A true friend. She laughed with me as well as cried as we moved through the next years together.

She was with me when I met a new love of my life who my brothers promptly nick named "Deputy Dog" because he was a sheriff for San Diego County and, like them, a former Marine. It was an unusual experience to date someone who always had a gun with him and was always on the alert for trouble. One day, we went to an outdoor concert and he told me someone was smoking pot. Really, I never even knew what pot smelled like until then. Anyway he was always in a protective mode. I had never, ever experienced this behavior...actually just the opposite.

My new love, Deputy Dog, was also an elder in his church and a father to a young daughter before martial issues separated him from both. He was a rare man and a dream come true for me.

This dream was to be shattered when he decided, for the sake of his daughter, to return to his wife and try to make their marriage work. I was devastated. This time I didn't cry alone...D.J. was there to cry with me. I had been rejected again, but at least I wasn't alone.

Once again I moved forward. This time I buried myself in my work. I thought maybe if I worked hard enough the pain would go away. The pit was becoming deeper and darker.

I found that saying true: *time heals*. It also helped to have friends who were there to distract me. One even set up a blind date for me and *viola!* Jon entered my life. Jon introduced me to a whole new life that I had no knowledge of before him. As a former Navy man, he now worked again for the Navy as a civilian and was remodeling a two-story home he had just purchased. When the top floor was complete, he planned to rent it out while working on the ground floor. I learned what it meant to live in a construction zone when I moved in with him…extension cords and tools everywhere. I also learned what various kinds of marijuana smelled like, too, and how a dealer worked his trade through Jon's friend, G.I., who was our upstairs renter. My angels must have been on high alert, no pun intended, as they worked to keep me safe, my job secure and my life intact.

Jon and I were good together. We laughed a lot, completed one another's thoughts and were able to say a word or two and have a complete conversation, leaving those around us baffled. We entertained a lot. Life was good. It was fun. Light bubbled down into my pit. But, these bubbles burst when Jon started traveling on assignments overseas, G.I. moved out, and D.J. and her husband moved to El Paso. There I was, alone again.

The walls of my pit were closing in on me. I knew what this compression felt like and didn't want to experience it again, so when D.J.'s husband asked me to come and work for him in his new hospital, I quickly said yes. *Yeah!* I was moving forward again.

This time I packed up and moved myself to El Paso in a U-Haul van with my car in tow. *Jon's plane could land in El Paso just as well as it could in San Diego, right?* At least this was my thought at the time. Needless to say things didn't work out that way.

When Jon and I parted ways, I wasn't as devastated as I had been in the past. Perhaps it was because I was now surrounded by friends and was emotionally adopted by a kind family. I belonged somewhere. I had a new identity. Yes, Phyllis and Clyde, an older couple, opened their hearts and their home to me as one of their daughters. Oh my gosh…I was loved for who I was, not what I could do! I was loved unconditionally. This was truly a new experience. Light once again filtered into my pit.

But like before, it was to be dimmed when Clyde died unexpectedly and Phyllis began her journey into Alzheimer's. In order to cope, I found myself going back into old patterns of survival. I threw myself into my new role: healthcare consulting. My work required moving to

Austin and then to Dallas, but the truth is I was running; running from pain. I had lost my new, caring family; the family that loved me and covered me with warmth and security. I was alone again. But at least I was in a new and exciting career. I was grieving alone again and now moving into an unknown career. Fear and apprehension were emotions of the day. But I have to admit there were also feelings of excitement. I was a consultant! I was moving up the success ladder.

This new career put into play all of the experience I had gleaned from starting up hospital business offices. I now traveled all over the Western part of the United States meeting new people, experiencing new cultures, and solving problems in large metropolitan hospitals as well as small rural hospitals. I was definitely on the move.

It was in one of the really, really rural hospitals that I was sure I was going to be *tarred and feathered* as well as *run out of town*. The board of the hospital had risen up against the management company who employed me. They were not happy with anyone who represented the company. I was in the wrong place at the wrong time. It gave rejection a whole new meaning! To set the stage, you need to know I was sitting outside of the hospital's board room waiting to talk to the hospital administrator about how I could help his business office be more productive. From my seat I could hear the voices of the board members and our hospital administrator. They were shouting and all trying to talk at once. My company, and therefore me, seemed to be the main topic of this very heated discussion.

I got up and made a call to the home office to tell them the situation was escalating out of control. Their advice was to leave the hospital and come home. *Well, okay,* but that was easier said than done. Home was in Austin, Texas. I was in a small rural hospital in Wyoming...home of the state prison. Not only was it a small western town with board sidewalks, but it had only one plane that flew in and out once a day. I had to time my departure around it. With the orders of my boss ringing in my ears. I walked as calmly as I could out of the hospital, got into my rental car and drove to my motel room. There I packed up my suitcase, drove to the little airport, turned in the rental car and waited for the plane.

As I sat waiting for my plane to arrive I tried to ignore the hostile glances from airport employees. Nothing stays secret or quiet in small, rural towns. All strangers are noticed. All information is gathered about them. I was definitely not one of them and not welcomed.

A few hours later I found myself flying over the Rockies on my way to Denver, Colorado. I just left one of the most hostile environments I was to experience in all of my consulting years. Once again, the Lord made sure my angels were protecting me. (I am not being melodramatic here...this was a very serious situation. Later I learned that the hospital administrator had turned the hospital board and staff against the management company. I definitely was not welcome in this hospital!)

In spite of these experiences, life was good. Although it was full, it wasn't fulfilling. At the time, I didn't even recognize the difference. They seemed one and the same to me then. My deception was deeply camouflaged by being constantly busy, experiencing a life that few would ever have: stylish clothes, nice car, beautiful apartment and a great salary. Consulting had introduced me to *living on the surface* and traveling. I traveled constantly, formed no deep friendships, and was alone most of the time. I did, however, rack up lots of air miles – definitely a perk.

Another perk of consulting was power. When I walked into a facility, I walked in representing the company that managed them. My decisions could affect their continued employment. I could make life better or worse for them. Either way, being a consultant gave me great confidence.

I didn't know at the time that I was being prepared to understand what it's like to walk in power. Yes, my job carried worldly power only, but it *was* power. God had introduced me to it, and now He's teaching me to walk in His power not my own. I must confess I'm still learning, like a baby learning to walk: get up, walk, fall and get up again.

Now the power looks different. When I walk into a room, I believe the atmosphere changes because He has walked in with me. I want to walk in confidence; the confidence of knowing who I am in Him and whose I am. This revelation was to come years later, but I was stunned when I received it. I have been assured many times that *nothing* in our lives is wasted. God uses it all.

I wasn't aware of any revelations yet when I met and fell in love once again. He was a fellow consultant and a widower with three beautiful daughters. We both traveled a lot, but weekends were spent with his daughters at all of their activities.

Goodness, mothers and fathers are kept busy! I had no inkling of this kind of life, but fell head-long into it. Coming up for air at 9:00 pm to sit and eat dinner or have time to really talk was totally new to me. I was learning to live by someone else's agenda – a radical change for me. I had always lived by *my* agenda. With that in mind, I was devastated once again when he decided he wanted to date others. It shattered me. I worked with this man. I worked with his associates. I traveled to his hospitals. I could not go through a day without constant reminders of him.

The saying, "Don't dip your pen in company ink" is so true. It's agony when things fall apart. And fall apart, I did. Thoughts of suicide were ever present...*anything to stop this pain*. There were times I was trying to make it minute to minute, not hour to hour, or even day to day. I remember walking out to my car one evening and pulling the car door open. I was going to crash my car to kill myself and knew I could succeed. I wasn't even considering the innocents I might have harmed had I carried out my plan. For whatever the reason, I hesitated and returned to my apartment to curl up in pain on my bed and pray for dawn to come. My world was once again shrouded in rejection, loneliness and pain, so much pain. Would it ever end?

How do I survive this pain? What do I do? Well, I did what I had always done...move. I should say, run. I packed myself up again and ran to Houston to help D.J. and her husband manage 26 medical clinics. As a clinic manager, I was given the most difficult clinics to straighten out. It was a challenge, but by now I was all into challenges. Anything to help me forget the pain of rejection.

Speaking of pain, at this time I was trying to get physically fit. Pain comes with moving inactive muscles. That isn't a newsflash. What is a newsflash is that while doing sit ups, I managed to completely sever my rectus muscle. This muscle connects the upper torso to the lower and is about four inches wide and an inch thick.

The muscle was severed in half and was bleeding internally. Later, I became the subject for a medical paper, and was used as a teaching lesson to the interns who were on staff at this hospital while I was there. Last, but certainly not least, one of my physicians made the comment that I must have had angels looking out for me, because internal infection was a very real possibility. I did have angels looking out for me, they were working overtime!

Thankfully, I did not get an infection, but I did develop a major hematoma (blood clot) that took months of ultrasound therapy to dissolve. I was on my way to healing physically, and because I was healing so quickly I was rewarded with…drum roll please…more work.

Yep. More work. Since I had sorted out physicians, staff and other operational issues so well, the HMO I was working for asked me to go to a new market in San Antonio as their Chief Operating Officer. This time I was to open four medical clinics from the ground up in 120 days. This meant hiring physicians, staff, developing operational systems like payroll, record transfers, equipment, and more, plus host a regional meeting of all Prudential's Western Regional HMO's in San Antonio .

Can you see a disaster in the making? I was still healing from a major surgery. I had packed and moved to a new city. I had left all of my friends behind. I was facing the challenge of a lifetime. D.J., my soulmate friend never came to see me or called even though the phone calls were free. I was alone again, trying to survive and doing a *horrible* job of it.

I called her and left a message, explaining how bad things were by giving her an example she could relate to. My example was that I couldn't decide which wall to put a painting on in my office. There were only three walls to choose from, and she would know this was odd and not typical of me. One of my passions was interior decorating. I had even flown several times to her various homes in the last 12 years to unpack her and decorate her home. The fact that I couldn't hang up one painting was a huge indicator of my unstable state of mind. She didn't respond, didn't come and didn't call. I truly felt like a nail had been pounded into a cover over my pit. Darkness was hurling in from all sides.

Darkness and anger were now elements of the day, almost all day, every day. I wanted it to end. *How much longer can this go on?* The answer came at the death of a truly wonderful friend in Houston. Upon receiving the news, I dropped to my knees in my office and cried out to God. I was at my end. I had nothing more to draw on. I had nothing more to give. *How do I get out of this emotional hell hole I'm in?* I was right where God wanted me to be.

When all else failed me, I finally turned to the Him, the Source.

I went home to my beautiful empty apartment and found my Bible. Surely there would be some form of comfort and direction within its pages. I opened to Joshua and began to read Chapter 1 verses 5-9: "I will never leave you nor forsake you. Be strong and courageous...be very strong and very courageous. Be careful to obey. Be strong and courageous. Do not be terrified, do not be discouraged, for the Lord your God will be with you wherever you go." These words were soothing to my aching spirit and body. He would never leave me nor forsake me. Everyone else had. He would not. I clung to those words and finally began to recognize the pit I was in. *Now what do I do? How do I get out of it?*

A new door was about to open.

Chapter 2

My First Steps into Freedom

"Answer me when I call to you, O my righteous God. Give me relief from my distress; be merciful to me and hear my prayer... the Lord will hear when I call to him." **Psalm 4:1, 3**

I knew I needed professional help, so I sought it through Minirith-Meier and Associates, a group of Christian counselors in San Antonio.

I sat across the desk looking at the psychiatrist and his intern. I knew I was at the end of my life as I had known it. I said to them, "This is Operation Rescue Carol. If you can't do this, then it's all over but the shouting." I was dead serious and they knew it. It had taken great courage to come to this office and even greater courage to admit I couldn't solve this problem. I was tired, so tired of being angry. I was tired of doing what others said was the impossible. I was tired of being a Chief Executive Officer in a growing HMO. I was tired of hiring doctors and medical staff. I was tired of setting up all support systems to make four medical clinics in four different geographical sites functional. I was tired of not sleeping.

This had been my life for the last 120 plus days. I was tired. I was at the end of my resources. I knew I was about to slip over an edge into nothingness. I knew I needed help, so I looked at them waiting to hear how they were going to go about rescuing me. What was their Plan of Action (POA)? I had always had a POA for my life. Isn't that how everyone survives? *Just tell me what to do and I'll do it.*

So began my journey out of my dark and lonely pit. God began *lifting me out of the slimy pit, out of the mud and mire* (Psalm 40:2). Although I didn't recognize it then, this was to be my first day of stepping into freedom.

Freedom was another big word for me; a *giant* word. It was a word that seemed easy for everyone else to say and feel...not so for me. My whole life had been about survival, *not* freedom. Oblivious to the work and sacrifice to come, at the time I was numb to everything. I was on the edge of insanity mentally and physically.

As with any rescue operation, background facts had to be gathered. Sitting in this psychiatrist's office was no different. With care and concern in his voice, the doctor began asking questions and gathering information. He began to get a glimpse of what had transpired in my life up until then. I stress the word *glimpse* because I hadn't been dwelling on the past and probably forgot a few things at that moment. I began to tell him of alcoholic parents, sexual abuse in the home, pregnancy, and later the adoption of my son, suicidal thoughts, alcoholic husband, divorce, becoming a leading medical/hospital consultant, major life-threatening surgery, moving to a new city, leaving all my friends behind, and my current task of opening four medical clinics and hosting a Western Regional Conference. The doctor looked at me in astonishment and, with a serious tone, said, "You have had incredible coping skills." My matter-of-fact response was, "Well, I guess I need new ones, because they aren't working for me anymore."

I wasn't trying to be *cute* or anything. This was serious. Many others who have endured and survived many major life events like mine turn to drugs or alcohol in order to cope. Thankfully, I didn't go in that direction. Instead I turned to *me* and *my strength* and built some pretty impressive walls of defense around me...that's what you do when you're an overachiever, A.K.A. a work-alcoholic.

My goal was always to be perfect at whatever I did. That was an unrealistic expectation, so I tempered it with high work performance, leading to over achievement. As a healthcare consultant, I was excellent. I wrote articles for national trade magazines, spoke at national conferences, developed standard guidelines for accessing the accounts receivables of hospitals, clinics and doctor offices, and traveled to many hospitals and clinics across the United States. If a checklist existed for high work performance or over achievement, I would check off all the boxes. *Surely I can find acceptance if I perform so well. Surely my walls should come down.*

There was a problem...I didn't realize I had erected the walls around myself. I was fully aware that the emotional place I was in seemed impossible to get out of no matter how hard I tried. It was like I was handcuffed to the walls of my pit by golden handcuffs, bound by money...nice amounts of it. The more money I made the more my lifestyle went up, and the more money I needed to maintain it. The cycle seemed never-ending.

It's hard to take golden handcuffs off. *How would I survive? Where would I live? What would I do? Who would I be without this status?* The more I succeeded, the darker my pit became. Life lied to me by saying, "the more I succeeded, the brighter my world would become." Too many people believe this dark lie about fame, status, money and instant gratification. By believing it, my world became darker. Where sunlight should have been pouring in continuously, I only received sporadic moments of light in the form of momentary laughter or brief glimpses of joy. Most of the time my pit was colored by anger, and I was getting very, very weary of being angry. However dark the pit was, it protected me and it was comfortable, or so I thought. The walls were now crumbling, and my psychiatrist was tasked with helping rebuild my world. Whatever that meant.

Rebuilding began after the initial *fact gathering stage* was done. Getting me to sleep was his first goal. I finally learned why sleep is vital to not only our minds, but our bodies. Without it, everything begins to crumble and our challenging circumstances begin to feel overwhelming and take on a bigger reality than they really are, leading to physical problems. I had failed to tell him I was taking six to eight Vicodin pain pills a day for severe back pain pending a much-needed back surgery. Only by the grace of God I did not become addicted. But I was still in daily pain, mentally and physically.

The second step in the doctor's plan was to help me calm my mind so I could begin to think clearly again. My *normal* had been wakeful anxiety with my mind racing at night, pouring over all that had to be done. It seemed to move a mile a minute, never shutting down. Achieving these first two goals was not easy. It included a lot of trial and error before the right combination of medications were found, but find them we did.

Even as this trial and error period was going on, I was still CEO and organizer of the Western Regional HMO's Conference. Approximately 200 attendees were coming to San Antonio, and it was my job to make sure they enjoyed their stay. Rooms were reserved in a beautiful hotel along the River Walk area of the city. A mariachi band greeted everyone the first evening and a Mexican buffet was laid out before them. In their rooms they received a gift – a sombrero whose rim was covered with assorted chips and dips all wrapped up and waiting for them on their beds. It was a huge success. I should have been ecstatic, but instead I was shattered and numb on the inside.

However successful the conference had been and the start-up of the four clinics, I was headed for yet another blow. This one came as medical directors were changed in San Antonio and the new director wanted his own Chief Operating Officer. I was asked to leave. *What?* I had poured my life literally into doing the impossible. Doctors, staff and systems were all in place. I had even started writing a monthly newsletter. *My reward is termination?* I felt the bottom of my world had fallen out beneath me. Now I was unemployed, isolated and feeling totally insignificant.

My psychiatrist certainly had his work cut out for him. I completely trusted that he could lead me through what seemed to be an endless nightmare. Imagine my shock when I walked into his office for my regular appointment and he told me he was moving to the East Coast. Operation Rescue Carol had just taken a major, direct hit. I was stunned. *Now what?*

The foundations of my already shaken world were shaken even more. Was it about to collapse entirely? Was I about to go over the edge? Was there a reason to go on? Walking out of his office, I was totally unsure of how to go forward from there. All my hope felt like it had just slipped out of my grasp.

But unbeknownst to me, my Heavenly Father was already at work to answer my questions and offer the safety net my life greatly needed. He had already been setting into motion events that led me to *Healing of the Nations*, a unique counseling opportunity in Colorado Springs. This was to be an intensive healing time, covered in prayer, and included individuals from all over the United States.

In this beautiful environment, I began to be set free from some of my anger and all the expectations I had of my best friend…my soul-mate friend who had never called or come to see me during this period of hell on earth. *Aren't friends someone you could count on when dark times come?* My best friend was still MIA.

Getting a taste of healing gave me a better sense of the long, long road I still had ahead of me in this journey. I wasn't confident I had the strength or endurance it would surely take. But, I was right where God wanted me – broken and desperate, open to His work.

In this surprisingly peaceful place, God began healing the broken pieces within me. Where I was emptied out, He began filling. Now, that I was away from all the distractions and was sleeping well, I began to hear God speak to me and experience His love for me. A book I once read called *The Green Letters*, said that "He gently pursues us with His love." It's true. He knew exactly what I needed: gentleness. He was gently pursuing me. I didn't need to be pushed. I needed to be gently led.

Together God and I left Colorado Springs and returned to my home in San Antonio. I packed and stored most of my things, placed basic essentials into my car and returned to Houston. I had no plan of action, I was just going through the motions. With nowhere to go, because it was New Year's Eve, I ended up in a friend's spare, empty apartment on an air mattress watching a portable TV. Me and my faithful kitty, Jasmine, were now homeless and directionless. *How much lower could I go?*

A new year was beginning, as was a new chapter of my life. New Year's Eve...how appropriate. What was the next step? *God, what do I do?* I certainly was in no shape to work. *Where will I live? How do I survive?* I could almost hear Him say, "Hush, Child. I've got this all worked out. Just trust me." Trusting without a plan didn't suit me well, but I had no other option. I had to trust Him. I had to lean in on Him. I was right where He wanted me. Right where I needed to be.

A year earlier while I was in Houston and attending Kingsbridge Christian Church in Sugarland, the women's ministry were creating prayer partners. I said I would like to have one, and they put me in touch with a woman named Suzanne. She and I had kept in touch when I was promoted to Chief Operating Officer and moved to San Antonio. During one of our weekly telephone calls, I shared how weary and broken I felt. It was Suzanne who saw the danger I was in and was the one who encouraged me to seek professional help. I had kept her updated with all that was happening, and now I wanted to call and let her know about my current predicament: I was in

Houston unsure of what, when, where, or how to go forth from this point.

God once again showed me that His hand was all over my life. Suzanne asked me to move in with her. What I hadn't mentioned is that her professional expertise was to work with mentally and/or physically challenged individuals. I felt like I fit the bill! God had placed me with the perfect person to begin my healing. He even gave me the perfect therapy: repainting every wall in her entire home…instant gratification…instant results…I love decorating, and viola! Therapy! All I needed to do was to cooperate with God, and cooperate I did. With every brushstroke, I expressed my heart to Him. Those many hours and days turned into precious alone time with my Father God, finding purpose and safety.

Thankfully Suzanne knew of a skilled, Christian therapist who I began seeing. I was not easy for the therapist because of my deep wounds and anger. I remember one particular day when, for the first time, she sat in her winged back chair, behind her big desk to begin our session. Why she did that on that day, I have no idea. I just know it triggered my anger.

I had finally reached a point in my healing that I could verbalize when I was upset, and so I verbalized. "Your chair, you sitting in it, and your desk represents abusive authority to me and if we are to go forward, I need you to sit beside me, not behind a desk." She responded with,

"Okay," and said we had to work on that issue. I said something to the effect, "Yes, but not right now." We moved on from there.

Her plan for helping me heal was to give me what seemed like endless books to read. Self-help books were not my cup of tea, but if this is what I needed to do in order to heal, I'd read them. I also found myself reading my Bible and journaling. God was becoming my true Healer. Journaling became my healing time. During these quiet times I would tell Him what I was feeling, what I was reading in His Word and the most exciting thing, what I believed He was saying to me. Those have been the most precious times.

God was healing me from the inside out. I was learning that He only asks us to do one step at a time...nothing more...*just one step at a time.* Even when I didn't outwardly see myself taking a step, He would encourage me, telling me He knew my heart and to keep going.

Apparently others did see the changes. I was asked to speak at a women's retreat. Frightened beyond what words can express, I said yes and turned frantically to my Father. *What do I say? How do I say it?* He answered my questions by taking me back to notes I had taken from one of the many books I had read called *The Wounded Heart*.

I began writing things down, and the next thing I knew it was complete.

Even as I write this today, I'm stunned by the enormity of His plans for us. "No eye has seen, no ear has heard, no mind has conceived what God has prepared for those who love him" (1 Corinthians 2:9). I put my name at the beginning of this verse, "Carol, your eyes have not seen, your ears have not heard, your mind has not conceived what I have prepared for you." This was mind blowing and still is. What is He up to? The answer to that question is still revealing itself, but like I did then, I do now...I move forward, one step at a time.

Speaking at this retreat was a major milestone in my journey. Because it was so impactful for me, I want to share it with you. These are the actual notes from my presentation. Amazingly, it outlines what transpired in my life with Him over the next 17 years.

> **Introduction:** My topic is short and, for me, painful. I stand before you in obedience to the message God gave me while I was going through my own quest to find out what grace is all about. God also showed me that I must tell each of you what I need from you in order to truly heal the wounds inflicted upon me. This isn't easy, because I've spent a lifetime not asking for any of my needs to be met. I now need your honest love, and concern, warm hugs, acceptance of the true me as I begin emerging. I need your understanding and encouragement.
>
> **Opening Prayer:** Lord, God, use this time as

spiritual bread for others who have felt as I have and still sometimes do, I pray the words I speak will glorify Your name. I pray they will be received and handled with love. For You, and You alone Father, know how vulnerable and fragile I am at this point in our journey. Lord, tug at their hearts and help them to be honest with themselves, for You have taught me that this is the first step towards embracing Your Grace. Father, You have shown me You love us too much to allow secrets, which result in anger, despair and shame. We thank You for that love and this time together. May each lady here take one more step towards becoming the whole child You want her to become. May we each leave this retreat having embraced Your grace to its fullest. We pray this prayer in the name of Your Son.

Broken and Spilled Out: Some of you heard my testimony about three years ago. Since that time, I have taken an honest look at myself, and what I saw was not a pretty sight. For the first time in my life, I looked at my childhood and the events which shaped me into the super-achieving, professional woman I've become. Where I once appeared as a happy child, I now see a child who had to achieve A's in order to get her parents' attention. Love was missing. Where others said they saw a beautiful girl turned woman, I saw a defective, flawed, shamed victim of incest. I was a young girl who became a victim of her father's and three brothers' incestuous behavior. Until February of last year, I had denied and hidden it.

What caused me to bring it to light? A series of things that led me to a Christian therapist who gave me these words: "Carol, you need to learn to embrace God's Grace." I remember numbly nodding my head "yes" and leaving. I didn't know that 15 months later I would be standing before you, telling what I have learned about God's grace.

My dear sisters, the most important thing I want you to hear is what our Lord has taught me as my life laid broken and spilled out before Him. He has gently brought me to see that His grace was made available to me when His own Son hung on the cross, broken in body, with His blood spilling out. He has shown me that grace is His never-ending mercy, love and generosity. This love has been hard for me to understand and trust, but I'm learning to trust the certainty of God's grace. It seems to come as unexpected, undeserved "love bursts."

As I look back in my life, I see evidence of grace even before I knew Him as my Savior. When I was a child of four or five, I asked my mommy if I could kneel and pray, or when He somehow gave me the image of Himself as a loving and compassionate Father. I've clung to that image for my entire life, even though I didn't fully understand it. He led me to find a church when I was ten years old. I went by myself, ladies, a pretty tough thing for an insecure little girl. But go I did, and I continued to seek Him at different churches all through Junior High and High School. That was His grace, unexpected and free.

Now that He is my Savior, He shows me His grace through the presence of the Holy Spirit and His Word. Please listen intently, see how this story applies to your life, and see the love and concern He has for us. He genuinely cares for you, like a Father should...not like how an earthly father or some other male figure may have mistreated you.

His love, concern and grace is so deep that He tells us in Psalm 56:8 that He records all of our tears. I must have volumes lining one whole side of heaven! He is teaching me that I must put grace into action by showing others love, compassion and understanding. Yes, the Fruit of the Spirit. It has come to me that our level of belief and acceptance of God's grace is directly related to the extent we express the Fruit of the Spirit. I've also been shown that God's grace is another word for blessings, and it can overshadow any guilt, fear, anger or shame we have within us. We must share it. We must accept the full measure He wants to give us.

Accepting anything from anyone has been extremely

difficult for me. As a child I learned to depend only upon myself and to always be on guard...never relax. I learned to be distrustful of others and their intentions. My work became my identity, and even now it's keeping our kitchen floor mopped and waxed. I began to overeat. I learned to fear rejection and men. Later it became clear I was a very angry person and had turned it all inward.

Ladies, these are some of the strongholds I unknowingly allowed Satan to put on me. He brought them to full bare when I went to San Antonio as the Chief Operating Officer, to build, furnish and staff four health care centers in 120 days. Like the Israelites who wouldn't go into the Promise Land with God, so I set forth without keeping God first. The result? A major clinical depression, which robbed me of my physical, as well as my mental health. Exhaustion from working 8 am to 10 or 11 pm seven days a week, left no time for anyone or anything else. I had placed myself in a prison – an isolated desert. Like prisons, which strip everything away, the prison of my mind stripped away my self-confidence, my identity, and left me in darkness, despair and hopelessness.

I couldn't seem to please my medical director. As an older, gray-haired man, I later realized I was seeing him as my father and was trying to please him. Nothing I could do was good enough. The Carol whose identity was wrapped up in her job performance began to break into thousands of pieces. It was then the gift of God's grace bore into my prison and began to minister to me.

I had totally rejected myself. I am still searching for who I am. The years of loneliness, grief, hurt and hopelessness are melting away in the strong embrace of God's love and grace. It has been a slow journey to gain back my health. My character is beginning to take on a new depth. I am being refined. I've realized that I must first be a willing servant to my Heavenly Father. Pleasing Him and Him alone is my only aim. Whereas fellow humans will let us down, He never will. He will only hold me in arms of love and whisper sweet words of comfort and love.

He will bless me and honor my plea to break the cycle of shame that has ensnared my family and me.

The shame stops here. I plead with each of you who have experienced anything similar to my story, to seek God's grace and stop your cycle. Please don't pass it on to your children and grandchildren.

Psalm 147:3 says that He heals the brokenhearted and binds up their wounds. Are you feeling broken? There is comfort in the words of 1 Peter 5:7 – "Cast all your fears and anxiety upon Him for He cares for you." Comfort for me was also found in Isaiah 43:18-19. "Forget the former things, do not dwell on the past. See, I am doing a new thing. Now it springs up, do you not perceive it? I am making a way in the desert and streams in the wasteland." My translation of these verses goes something like this:

What has happened has happened. Don't dwell on it.

For me, part of the former things include the violation of my innocence and the anger which resulted.

You, Lord, are molding me into a person with new thoughts, new emotions. Love, understanding and compassion are beginning to replace the anger. The NEW ME is pushing upward through the crust of the old me. You, Lord, in your infinite grace are in control of the pushing. I can see it!

Right now, You Lord, are creating a path of escape from this desert of despair/depression by filling me with your living waters of love and grace. You are eroding away the lifeless, barren, unloving, angry part of my wasteland. What is slowly emerging is a new me.

Time and time alone will cause the total erosion of the wasteland, which was once me, and the creation of living water which will flow from me.

Are you ready to ask our Father to continue the erosion of your wasteland?

Are you ready to take the next step in becoming the free and whole child He wants you to be?

Closing Prayer: I am humbled once again, my Lord, that You love me so much to use this painful story to help my sisters. As you brought Your Word, Your manna to me when I was a prisoner in the desert, You will also bring it to those who accept Your words in Joshua to be strong and very courageous. It takes courage to come to that moment of honesty, where we see the truth about ourselves and become vulnerable to Your unexpected grace. We trust You to treat us gently as we choose freedom…freedom to be the healthy whole child You created us to be. In Your Son's precious and holy name we pray, amen.

I know I'm being redundant, but I have to stress again, that this was the *outline for my new life*. I really didn't know how deep God and I were going, but I knew I was being obedient. Obedience: the big "O" word. To stand before a group of women and tell them what I needed was a sign that Operation Rescue Carol was working.

At the time I thought I was setting myself up to be rejected. Sadly, their response to what I had to say was a form of rejection. No one responded to my need. But this time it was okay. I had grown close enough with God that I wasn't devastated, and the words a friend had told me earlier had stuck. She advised me not to tell them everything, because they wouldn't know how to deal with it. Maybe she was right. They didn't know how to respond…they didn't even when I told them how to. I just know that I was obedient to what God told me to say. He hasn't asked me to say it again until now, 20 years later.

Being broken is painful. Going back into my pit was painful. Healing can be slow. I knew then and I know more so now, that I never want to go through the intense healing season again. I wanted to learn what I needed to learn and move forward. Who wants to be like the Israelites who went around the same mountain for 40 years? I wanted to go forward, and that I did.

This journey began in 1995 and here I am in 2017 sharing hope, truth and transformation with you. God can help us through anything. It's been a painful journey. If I said it was easy, I'd be lying. It has taken courage and perseverance. This one truth I knew from the beginning: I couldn't go back. I knew the hell that it had been. Forward was the only option…forward, one step at a time.

Chapter 3

Journey on the Mountain

"I will lead the blind by ways they have not known, along unfamiliar paths I will guide them. I will turn the darkness into light before them and make the rough places smooth."
Isaiah 42:15

Love pulled me out of my pit...His love. In one of my journals I wrote, "Lord, we have been in this pit." And my heart felt His gentle reply, "Oh Child, you have been trying to climb out under your own power. I must be your Power, your Strength. Give up. Let me do the work. Remember the harness?"

Ah yes, I remembered the harness. I remember writing that You had met me in the pit...You showed me Your light was not just on the rim of my pit, available if I were somehow able to reach it, but it was *with me* in the pit.

You led me thru the valley of the shadow of death. You put Your safety harness around me and began leading me up the mountain of transfiguration, my transfiguration. You began transforming me, one step at a time. You told me the Holy Spirit was my ever-present harness...Your Word was the tether between us. You said, "Yes, we are climbing a mountain together. Put your cleats in deep.

You are roped to me. I won't let you fall. Even though you may swing out, you won't fall. My rope and hands are enough. Yes, I am enough. Always keep reminding yourself of that. I am enough."

He told me to write these thoughts down, because I would need them in the future. I had no idea this was the future He was referencing. *Yes, indeed I remember the harness. I remember the climb. I remember our experiences.*

I remember the caves on my mountain and sometimes dwelling in them until hearing Him tell me to come out and start climbing again. Thank you, God, for asking us to take only one step at a time. Remember, I had been running my entire life…to walk was a new lesson. To walk forward, fall, and get up was all new.

Also, I didn't need to be perfect. *What? Really?* That realization was so freeing when I finally learned it. No overachieving or perfection required! I could just be me and focus on listening to and pleasing Him…not everyone or anyone else. This was one of the most freeing lessons I was to learn.

Sometimes when I was in a cave, I was frozen while there. Why was I frozen? It's really simple: I was overwhelmed by what I was being asked to go through…I couldn't move. But do you know that frozen things melt when they come in contact with warmth? I melted when I came in contact with the Son and His love. Living water flowed from me and splashed onto anyone nearby. My healing was bringing about the new me; the real me who God created originally!

Sometimes on this journey up the mountain, God would pick camping sites rather than caves to teach me. I have to admit camping isn't my thing, but I was willing to learn. I found out He makes everything a sweet experience – even camping, and earthquakes. I learned that He uses the earthquakes to break off chains still clinging to me.

He sees progress even in the small steps. He knows when I could only move an inch at a time, and that inch would become a mile. I've thanked him many times for His faithfulness as I learned to stand and walk in Him. Again, when I fell, He would pick me up, dust me off and encourage me to take the next step.

Yes, He was definitely pursuing me with His love. At times He desired my freedom more than I did. He was removing me from my old life and drawing me closer to Him and His abundant life. The old has gone, the new was coming. I was moving from surviving life to living life; His thriving, joyful life.

I have to admit there were times when I felt blind. *Where are we going? How will we get there?* Even as I asked these questions, He led me to the answers. It came to me in Isaiah 42:15: "I will lead the blind by ways they have not known, along unfamiliar paths I will guide them. I will turn the darkness into light before them and make the rough places smooth." God is well able to be my guide. My road to healing definitely took me down unfamiliar paths. Sometimes they appeared to be threatening and very dark, but if I clung to Him, He would patiently, lovingly lead me through. The rough places did become smooth.

As an example, I want to share another excerpt from one of my journals. Read it and see the loving heart and hand of our Father. See His patience for me to get to the place He wanted me to get. See my reluctance. See my blind eyes open.

Esther – It's Tough Being a Woman

At church we began a Bible study on the book of Esther in January, 2009. Esther is the story of a Jewish woman taken from her family by a king; a king who gathered the most beautiful women in his kingdom in order to choose the best one for his queen. After choosing Esther to be queen, the king signed a law that would destroy her Jewish nation. But, God used her, miraculously, to save it. She was in the king's house "for a time such as this."

I started by telling you we began the study in January, 2009. I repeated the same study in April 2009. As I put thoughts down on paper the first month, I didn't see the whole message. It wasn't until the last session in April that I got a picture from God about the similarities between Esther's life and mine. It took me until June to finally sit down with my journal and a pen to talk with God about it more.

Lord, help me to connect the dots and show me what You want to say. There must be a powerful word here for me. Sorry You are dealing with me: one stubborn person. He said, "No, Child, I am dealing with a deeply wounded child. I want you to heal, to be restored. I have much for you to do."

The following is my journey of discovery through Esther (my journal excerpts).

> It has been a fight. I want to say a battle. A battle I didn't win the first time through the study. But I realize it is a battle to stop existing and start living. It is a battle to live as a free child of God. I am a Warrior Bride. Discovering who I am as a woman is a battle.
>
> I realize I have been the prodigal daughter who has squandered money, time and resources. I'm returning to You, Lord, empty handed and so wounded. "I know child. I am here to heal all of those wounds and to restore you. I am covering you with My healing Spirit."
>
> You are changing my roles at home. Where I have always been the leader, You are now asking me to be a follower. I am trying Lord, and it is so painful. I

feel like I am losing another part of me. "You are, Child. You are dying to yourself. This is good."

You're telling me that we are going deep and not to hold my breath. It's time to take off the floaties of *I can do this myself,* and *I don't need anyone.* These floaties have kept me on the surface. This is scary, Lord, terrifying! "I know, Child, hold on tight. I won't let anything harmful happen to you. You are precious to Me."

We have been learning about Esther's childhood, and I realized that like her I, too, have been an orphan. I am an emotional orphan. Mom and Dad didn't know how to love us or teach us how to live. They provided food and shelter and that was all. I had to learn how to survive on my own, and without a biblical compass for my foundation. Without this compass and its principles, I developed negative attributes and couldn't see God in the camouflage of my existence.

I know I've been hidden for a time such as this…a time to begin changing the negative attributes into positives. I am trusting, Lord for the negative to be changed to reflect Your glory. If I don't trust You, believe You, then all is lost. There is no reason to go forward.

You are attracted to my weakness…here I am with

so many weaknesses that I don't know where to start! Lord, even as I write this, I feel so utterly overwhelmed and afraid that I'll miss Your instructions. "Stop fearing, Child. I have You safely in the palm of My hand. I am the Lord your God...nothing can take you away from Me. Look back and see. Notice how I have kept you from harming yourself. See that you have been hidden. We will make this journey together. Just hold tight. Cling to me."

Lord, the tears are streaming down my face as I hear Your words. I know You are speaking the truth and it will set me free. My flesh is in a major battle right now. Surround me, Lord. Surround me with Your Holy Presence. I know I need to complete this and I know it will be a battle. "I am here, Child. Your angels surround you. They will protect you. Push on."

You are telling me to walk in who I am in You, to stay close to You. As I just wrote this, I remembered the revelation You gave me, that I am totally surrounded by the three aspects of You: Father, Son and Holy Spirit. I am triple insulated! I must remember to take this truth deep within me for the battle ahead. I know that it's crucial to my growth and to my becoming the Warrior Bride You have created me to be. Lord, I have written in my Bible in Esther, "Keep pressing out, Lord, as I press in."

Lord, I know You are inside of me and You are wanting me to be more like You. I know that I can only be what You created me to be by pushing myself to be in Your word more and more. When I am there You reveal yourself more and more and I begin changing more and more. This too, is a battle. So many things want to distract me from sitting down quietly and listening for Your voice.

I haven't wanted to put my toe back into the water of life (much less dive in without floaties), and You've instructed me not to hold my breath.

I have worn sackcloth around my heart...a sackcloth of grief. It's time to take it off and to shatter the shackles that have come with it. One of those shackles has been fear. You want me to be confident in You, to cling to You. "Rise up, Carol. Enter the courts of the King. You are a child of royalty. I love you." This is Your command! Give me the courage and the perseverance, Lord.

In order to rise up I need help identifying my concerns and feelings. They've been buried so long. They had to be buried in order to survive. I believed that to let them surface would mean my destruction. "Let them rise, Child. We need to destroy their power over you. I have freedom and a new power for you. My power." Lord, then You need to help me identify them and articulate them, and then to apply truth to them.

You're telling me that You are mighty to save, that You are the Lifter of and Repairer of my heart, to put on my royal robes of righteousness and to step out confidently and boldly. Step up in faith. You will change my sadness and grief into joy and gladness. Lord, I am clinging to those words. They are words of hope and life.

I feel like I am drowning. "You aren't, Child. I have you surrounded. Remember that in moments like these." Thank you Lord for fighting for me.

Lord, I have completed the task You gave me and I can hardly contain myself. Your words of encouragement, instruction and hope are now written for me to return to time and time again. Thank you, Lord, for urging me to sit down and complete this assignment. Thank you for Your endless patience with me. You know that I've been afraid to write them down. To write them made them a reality and the flesh side of me wasn't sure I wanted that reality. But, You are faithful to hear our prayers and to answer them. Continue having Your Kingdom invade my world, Lord, until all that I am is Yours.

I love You, Lord. I love You. As much as I know of love right now, I love You. "I know, Child, I know.

Keep seeking. You will find, I promise. I have given others to come along side of you in your journey, so let them help. They are My hands, My love reaching out to you. Embrace them."

Did you see His love for me? Did you see the constant encouragement? The battle I was in was real and painful. Healing doesn't happen overnight.

I'm so thankful for my church; a church that believed in healing the spiritually wounded. Indeed, I was wounded. A very good friend of mine described the church as a spiritual Emergency Room. I described it as a spiritual Intensive Care. God had brought me to the perfect place and surrounded me with loving and caring people; people who were passionate about helping others find their freedom in Christ and who they are in Him. They were also passionate about helping the body to grow in their relationship with the Lord – to have a relationship with Him, not just a religion.

For me the healing continued just as He had foretold at the women's conference many years ago. Remember when I said, *"I am still searching for who I am. The years of loneliness, grief, hurt and hopelessness are melting away in the strong embrace of God's love and grace. It has been a slow journey to gain back my health. My character is beginning to take on a new depth. I am being refined"*?

Indeed it was a slow journey to healing and refinement,

but it was in this spiritual intensive care unit where I really began to put all the pieces together. As a disciple, I had found myself in a customized mentoring program where I read books like *Tired of Measuring Up* and *The Normal Christian Life,* watched videos like *Victory Over Darkness* and *The Life*, listened to Joyce Meyer CDs on *Wilderness Mentality,* wrote what God was speaking to me, and shared with my mentor. His truth was pouring into me from all directions. I finally began to understand who I am in Christ.

To enhance this new awareness, I signed up for a two-day intensive called Cross Encounter. Does that give you a clue? I was about to have an encounter with the Christ of the Cross. This intensive teaching was covered constantly in prayer. God made His presence known to each of the participants and as well as to the teachers. I can tell you that it was a watershed moment for me. I believe God had been at work months before to get me ready for this moment. I don't even remember why I wrote the following, but I can tell you that it shows His careful preparation, His encouragement and His protection.

A Confirmed Pit Dweller

Before I tell you about Cross Encounter and its impact on me, I need to give you some background as to what led up to it. Remember that God is always preparing us for the next step we will be taking. These steps were no different.

In May 2007, I started working at The Home Depot in the décor, flooring and paint departments. I loved working with the customers, helping them make decisions regarding their home interiors, learning about flooring and sharing in their joy when they came back in and told me how beautiful their project had turned out. As you know, decorating was a passion of mine. Without going into great detail, suffice it to say I learned more about authority and submission at that job than I thought I would ever know. For example, I learned the corporate world was not always in line with the actual world.

Regardless of the misalignment, you are required to follow the corporate guidelines regardless of the negative impact they would have on your store. This made no sense to me coming from my previous background, but follow the guidelines I did. I learned fellow teammates in other department were very reluctant to help you pick up and move boxes in your department. I learned management seemed unable to solve this problem. I learned frustration and exhaustion resulted when collaborative needs were ignored.

Through being mentored, I recognized the hand of the Lord and knew I was being broken. My layers were thick, and I didn't realize how many layers we were going to peel off in 16 months. On September 4, 2008, I left work literally hysterical and drove to the church. WHY? I had nowhere else to go and knew no one who would even begin to understand what was happening to me. God's loving arms embraced me and soothed my aching heart. Wisdom was spoken into my spirit and I came home utterly exhausted both physically and emotionally.

I had one day to *get my act together* and get packed and prepared to travel to the Advance in Navasota. It was during this preparation time when I was about to immerse myself in a soaking tub full of lavender-scented bubbles when I heard, "Greater is He that is in me than he who is in the world. It startled me, and so I followed up with this question: "Am I letting my job become greater than You?" The answer was an immediate, "Yes." My response, "Can I think about this a moment?" "Yes," He answered. *Oh, my! Now what do I do?*

I slid down into the bubble bath and began meditating on the verse. *Greater is He that is in me.* One of my pastors, Pastor Anne, used the same verse at the Advance, and then there it was again from her husband, Pastor Rusty the Sunday we returned. Confirmation was coming from the outside of what I had heard on the inside. I knew this was to be a major verse in my life, if not my life verse. The Lord was doing a greater work in me. He was using the pastors at my church to reinforce what He was telling me. I was stunned to think I was hearing the same scriptures my pastors were hearing. Me, a deeply wounded child was hearing what seasoned/mature pastors were hearing. How could this be?

The work continued at the Advance with the message

centering on my being complete in Christ and the deposit of His spirit in me. It resonated throughout my being. How could I marry this message with the resounding fear that was overwhelming me; the fear that I'd miss what He wanted me to do? He had the answer ready for me during the Advance. I was prayed over by mighty women of God and was stunned by what I heard. In essence I was told anointing oil was dripping off of me, that I had led so many others through their maze and now it was my turn, and that God had me wrapped tightly in chicken wire. I went to bed with thoughts racing through my mind, but yet strangely at peace. Being wrapped in chicken wire was an extremely weird image to wrap my mind around…

The peace that passes all understanding was still with me when I returned to work the following Monday and turned in my resignation. Two weeks later, I was officially unemployed and waiting on the Lord for the next step. God kept saying, "Stand, watch, see what I can do."

In my journal I asked the question, "What is dead in my life?" The answer was unsettling. "Deep feelings and trust." *Wow.* I realized the truth in the answer, however unsettling it was. I had trained myself to keep emotions, relationships and trust on a superficial level. By doing so, I thought I could control being hurt. God was at work to show me not only the lie I had been living, but how much damage it had done.

His work continued the next day as I listened to Session 4 of the Restoration Tapes, where another one of my pastors, Pastor Nancy, said to "write down what God is pointing out, because death is on its way. And in Session 5, she said, "Faith it until I make it." I was writing, dying and "faith'ing" it. What now Lord? What now? During my quiet time with God I heard, "I'm here, Child. I'll always be here. Listen for Me. Cling to Me. I am enough. I am Jehovah Jireh. I am your Provider. I am your Protector, your Shield. Hide in Me and Me alone." Once again His words vibrated throughout my spirit. "I AM ENOUGH...I AM MORE THAN ENOUGH. I AM EL SHADDAI."

Now we approach the day before the Cross Encounter.

I knew I was heading for a major crash. God was preparing me for the next hurdle we had to overcome together. A couple of weeks later, I found myself emotionally strung tight as I went into mentoring. *What is wrong?* I couldn't put my finger on it, but when *it* was revealed, I almost ran out of the room. *It*, had a name; a name I very, very rarely said out loud. *It* was too painful. And then my mentor said *it*. There *it* was, out in the open, suddenly sucking all the air out of the room: *LONELINESS*.

I sobbed as *it* was spoken. I sobbed at the depth of loneliness in my life. I sobbed at the thought of its death and my potential freedom. *This could be the hurdle that takes me down.*

I left my mentor and the mentoring room with raw emotions. As I drove home, I found myself still sobbing and crying out to God...I felt like a nail had been driven into my coffin. Although it was isolating, loneliness had kept me from experiencing more disappointment and pain, or at least I thought it had. What kind of lifestyle would I have without the guard I had created at the age of four? Yes, I had prayed for God to be my rear guard, my shield, but now we were going into the very depth of the pit where I had dwelled for 58 years. His words began rising in my spirit. "Cling to me. I am your Protector, your Shield. Hide in Me and Me alone."

For the next 17 hours war raged within me. Suzanne came home from helping with preparations for the Cross Encounter and kept saying how awesome it was going to be. Every time she said it I felt another nail go into my coffin. Sleep was not to be had, as old relationships kept coming to mind. I prayed for God to remove the memories if they weren't being used by Him...they stayed...the nailing continued.

Dawn finally came and I approached the Cross Encounter location quivering inside, yet numb, excited, and yes, still fearful. My internal cry was, *Lord, deliver me from me...You are the only one who truly knows me.* A pressure was building inside of me and continued to build as *truth* began pouring in.

Truth revealed:

- I can't and haven't met any of my own basic needs.
- My fleshly ability to even try has been for naught.
- God did it all for me!
- I think more highly of myself than I ought.

"Child, I have given you what you desire more than anything in this world: love and a new family. I love you. See My arms around you. You are no longer alone. You are precious to me. I have heard the cry of your spirit deep within your pit. I have come to make all things new. I will raise you, Child, the way you should be raised. Raising from the dead is my specialty."

How could I resist those powerful words of truth and love? I almost ran to the cross and nailed my fears to it. The pressure I felt ceased, and the seed of freedom was not only erupting, but also sprouting roots as it did. For the first time in my life I felt the words *free* and *freedom* applied to me. I finally, truly received His life. *I am complete in Him! I am a warrior. In Your power I can do this life...Your life...my fears have been nailed to the cross.*

I AM NO LONGER RESTRAINED OR BOUND.
I AM NO LONGER A CONFIRMED PIT DWELLER.
I AM A PARTAKER OF YOUR LIFE.

I wish I could say that experience and declaration of who I really was made my life suddenly happy clappy, as someone once said. It wasn't immediately. I still had to work out what had been placed within me. Remember, it took decades of being in the pit with all the lies to mold me into the pit dweller I'd become. It would now take years for God to undo what Satan had done. I firmly believe that God can completely change us in a heartbeat. I also firmly believe He's allowed me to go through so many steps back to Him so I can understand and identify with the journey others might take. You know the saying, "Walk a mile in my shoes." Trust me when I say I've walked the mile and then some.

Chapter 4

Freedom Walk

"You will find in Me what you are looking for, Child. Keep seeking. I am what you seek."

God was destroying my shame, shattering my self-image and restoring me to be what He created me to be: a Partaker of His Life. I was a baby partaker. I even wrote, "I am sitting at Your table each morning when we study together and You feed me. I feel so like a baby, Abba Father. I feel like You are feeding me one spoonful at a time." In His gentle voice He said, "It's okay, Child, you're growing and you delight me with your eager heart. We have much to share. Let Me fill you to overflowing."

In a later journal I wrote, "I have found absolute favor with You, just like Mary, mother of Jesus. You're doing the impossible within me. You're birthing a new me. I feel like such a baby right now, crying. You birthed me, and I'm now trying to understand my new world. I'm getting a new perspective. Lord, grow in me a deep, deep childlike simplicity. You can and are restoring the child-likeness in me.

The truth is we all start out as babies in Him and then

begin growing. And like human babies, spiritual babies are all different. Because of that, God comes to each of His children in a very special way...a customized way...a way especially created just for you and Him. For me, He came to me during a time of worship. He came in the form of a vision. This is the only time He's given me one. Here it is:

> I was worshipping in church one Sunday morning, when I saw and felt Jesus lean over me and gently push me towards God the Father who was sitting on His throne. He made a "Go, baby, go" motion with His hands that parents do when they are encouraging their child to go towards something. As a child, I stepped forward and moved toward the Father. He leaned over, gently picked me up and put me onto His lap. I rested my head against His shoulder and drew a deep breath. I knew I was safe and secure...I was loved beyond my wildest imagination.

My Heavenly Father loved me. He loved me! I cannot even begin to tell you what that meant and still means to me. It brings tears to my eyes when I think of it still and causes my spirit to leap with joy. I can only urge you to stop right now, close your eyes and imagine it. Perhaps you will get a glimpse, too.

Since then, I've asked Him to give me more visions, but He has told me that I don't need them, that I hear Him instead. *Well okay...then anoint my ears to hear You and have the courage to be obedient to what I hear.*

Hearing Him has been such a blessing to me. He has told me that I hear Him because I *expect to hear Him*. That seemed simple enough, but however simple it is, I've sometimes wondered if I'm hearing Him or my own thoughts. I've asked Him that question while journaling, and He spoke to my heart. "You *are* hearing Me. I'm not distant. I'm right here. I'm holding you close, so very close. Your angels are surrounding you, protecting you. They aren't letting all the dark forces assigned to you through. Call for more. I will send more. You must speak to Me more. You need something from Me. You will use it." I asked "What do You want from me?" He said, "Your voice."

He wants my voice, my words! It's so amazing – the very thing that put me into the pit has not only brought me out of it, but is healing me, and I pray will begin the healing in you. I remember phrases like, "Smile and the whole world smiles with you. Cry and you cry alone." Well, that certainly seemed to have been true before. Or how about, "You made your bed, now lie in it?" All of my life I heard words like this from my mother, that is, until one day a friend of mine was speaking to me and said that I had an IV stuck in me, dripping all of the negative things my mother had said into me. She was right.

While driving home from my friend's house, I prayed and

commanded that IV out! I never wanted it to drip into me again. No, no more...lies were no longer going to be part of me. They were not what God wanted me to hear. He wanted me to hear only truth. He wanted me to learn new thoughts, new ways.

Learning new truths, thoughts and ways has been sometimes painful. I was journaling about one of those painful learning times, and once again He was there saying, "I hear you, Child. It's okay, you are being plowed right now...old ground is being crumbled. The seed I plant needs soft earth. Hard parts within you need to be broken. Yes, Child, it will be painful, but oh the fruit! Lean on Me. Cling to Me. I am enough. I will spread your wings, and you will soar like an eagle. You will rise above the dark valley you are in. I have much for you to do, and only you can do it. Rest, Child, I am doing the work. Just let Me."

Letting Him do the work has been the hardest lesson to learn. I learn it, and then need to relearn it and be reminded of it again and again. I find myself falling back into old behaviors of trusting myself, my agenda and skills. Maybe it isn't out loud with my words, but my actions say, *I've got this, God. I'll call You for the big stuff.* I'm so thankful He patiently lets me go my way, until things go awry and I finally call upon Him. He still comes, every time.

I now understand why God couldn't build on the

foundation I had. Instead, He has taken it all down and started from scratch. He's given me a new foundation, a new life…His life. The old Carol and her ways of doing life have died and continue to die. The process of dying to self is not a one-time deal, rather it's a life-time deal. Once again I can tell you that God uses customized ways to point out to us what needs to die or what He is trying to teach us. For me, one of His main tools has been the use of animals. I love all animals and could always trust them…people…ah…not so much. Let me share a few of my pet lessons with you and you will see some of what I mean.

Before I start, you should know that I didn't even realize my first lesson was a lesson from God. He would reveal the lesson to me as I journaled and prayed years later. Remember, *nothing* is wasted in your life. He will use it!

My first unannounced lesson started with Jasmine, my beautiful calico kitty. She and I had traveled from Dallas to Nashville, to Huntsville, Alabama, to Dallas again, then Houston, onto to San Antonio, and then back to Sugar Land, a suburb of Houston. She had seen me through hell and back. She was always there when I needed comfort, a soft coat to pet or a loving purr. She was to be the instrument God used to teach me to play.

I really didn't know how to play. She and I would play "chase" in my second floor apartment. She would run and I would be right behind her, until she stopped and looked back at me. That was my cue to turn around and run and let her chase me. I would even try hiding from her with absolutely no success! This would go on for at least an hour once or twice a week. It never entered my mind what my downstairs neighbors might be thinking. I was just having *fun*.

My beautiful Jasmine was hit by a car and killed one night in Sugar Land. My already wounded spirit was stabbed again. I remember collapsing on Suz's front lawn, holding my faithful friend and sobbing my heart out. Once again I was numbed by pain, and once again Suz was used by God to bring direction into my life. That direction came in the form of a suggestion to get another pet. It went in one ear and out the other.

But once again, time does heal, and one afternoon I went to a no-kill shelter. It was there that my beloved Hannah, a sheltie-chow mix dog came into my life. She had a long golden coat, big brown intelligent eyes and a bushy golden tail that curled over her back, and yes, the famous black tongue.

When I first saw her, I ignored her and picked up her litter mate instead. I had chosen another puppy, and as I picked up the puppy I glanced at Hannah. Something in her eyes made me stop, put down her litter mate and immediately pick her up. In retrospect, I truly believe Holy Spirit was at work. Hannah was His choice, so Hannah it was.

We were meant to be together and together we were. Hannah had so many beautiful qualities. Even as a puppy she would lay outside of the bathroom door guarding when I was bathing. She was always on guard to keep me safe. She was the top dog in our ever growing family of pets. She was the one who stood right beside me as we watched her favorite kitty friend, Leah, have her kittens. Hannah would not let the kittens mew without searching out Leah if she had left them for a moment.

She was special, very, very special. I knew she was, but really didn't understand how much, until the day I took her to the vet because she wasn't acting like herself. She stepped on the scales and to my horror, she had lost one third of her weight. It had been camouflaged by her long golden coat. I was stunned and then shattered when the vet gently told me that she had cancer of her tongue and there was no cure. She was starving to death. I took my beloved Hannah home to have one more night with her.

The next morning I returned to the vet and said goodbye to my faithful, loving friend. This is so hard to even write about...the tears are streaming. She was precious to me.

I journaled about her shortly thereafter, and as I journaled to God, I was asking Him what some words meant, like *grace* and *unconditional love*. Like a loving Father, he showed me picture cards in my mind – the kind that have the word on one side and a picture of the object on the other. When I asked Him what the word unconditional love looked like, He showed me Hannah. *Ah-ha!* I now had something in my life that I could relate His love to. I wept and wept.

If my Abba Father loves me that much, how can I not love Him in return? I knew how much I loved Hannah and He was showing me a portion of His love in a way I could really understand. It was a small-scale example of course, knowing that His love is so much more; more than can even be fathomed. I now know the depth of pain when a relationship of unconditional love is lost. Experiencing that depth was necessary in order for me to even begin to grasp God's love…a love so deep that He gave His Son's life for me. He even told me, "You gave up Hannah…it cost you. But look at what you learned; you learned about unconditional love. She was My gift to you and you learned what it looked like." This still takes my breath away.

I am totally convinced that God will show you His unconditional love in a unique and personal way, giving it deep meaning to you. It will be a life-changing experience, I can promise you that.

God was to teach me once again by using a little, white, deaf dog. But to understand the important lesson, I need to give you some background leading up to it.

Our church was studying John Bevere's book *Bait of Satan*. It's a book regarding the impact that offenses have on the

Christians. I was at home doing my homework in the workbook and had just written my definition of an offense:

"When someone or something interferes with my agenda."

Please note the "my." With that sentence down on paper, it dawned on me the little white deaf dog we were caring for temporarily needed to go outside. I have to admit I was slightly put out that *my* homework had been interrupted, but I got up, found her, and took her outside. Remember, I couldn't call her name...she couldn't hear, so this took more effort on my part to get the task done.

When she was done with her bathroom break, I brought her back inside, fussing internally to *myself* the whole way. All of a sudden I heard God ask me to spell God backwards. I did...d.o.g. With the last letter *g*, I fell on my knees. *Oh my gosh. This little, white, deaf dog just became an offense to me...*

I had set myself up as god of *my* agenda, *my* life and she had interfered with it. *What a jerk I'm being!* The shattering that went on inside of me was surprising. *My* pride had been brought to the forefront of *my* mind and it filled *my* entire being. The enormity of it was stunning. Actually I was hysterical over seeing it. *How could this be? How could I be so full of me, that a little, white, deaf dog offends me? Is my pride that all-consuming?* The answer was obviously *yes.*

What do I do? How do I change this, this enormous, ugly truth about myself? I was totally overwhelmed. *Where do I start?*

These were only a few of the questions racing through my mind as I went to bed and tried to sleep. Sleep did not come easily that night. First thing in the morning I woke up and called my church. They could surely help me. In tears and once again hysterical, I asked to speak to one of the pastors. An hour later I was sitting in her office trying to describe what had happened. In between the sobs I got out the event. In a calm, gentle voice she started speaking to me about what God was doing. I sniffed, blew my nose and tried to take in all she was saying. That was a difficult thing to do, but I heard what I know I was supposed to hear.

This is a paraphrase of what she said: God just revealed to me the enormity of my pride. It would have to die, but He didn't expect it to happen overnight or expect me to do all of the work alone. He would be in charge of making it happen in His time.

A wave of relief washed over me. I didn't have to be in charge of making my pride die – God would do it. He would work it out of me over time. I just needed to be in agreement and be aware of how many actions, words, thoughts, etc., were driven by my pride and not by Him. This is a never-ending lesson.

I and *me* are slowly being replaced with *Him, You* and *His*.

Self dies slowly. My pastor often says that in order for the good news to be really, really good, we have to see how bad the bad news really, really is. I had the opportunity to see and experience the depth of my really, really bad...all through a little, white, deaf dog. Who knew except God? The transformation in this area of my life is on-going as I'm learning to take up my cross daily...

Moving forward always brings new challenges and my journey is still full of them. Right now God and I are working on a stronghold of fear that has governed my life. I just journaled, "We're going further up the mountain, aren't we?" He said, "Yes, Child, we are. This will be a difficult climb for you, but I've got you. Don't lose sight of where we are going. Stay focused. It will be a rocky path. The rocks will try to dislodge you, make you stumble and fall. Remember the harness. No harm will come to you. Keep pressing upward." What can I do, except move forward? Going backwards is out of the question!

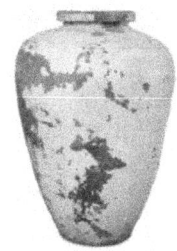

Chapter 5

The Healing Continues

"Let your face shine on your servant, save me in your unfailing love." Psalm 31:16

To move forward and climb upward requires faith and trust. Remember, trust was a scary word for me, but faith and trust are necessary to heal at one level in order to reach the next. This is not a *one time, one level* process. All of us will continuously be going from one level to the next until we're called home by God.

My faith walk started 17 years ago with baby steps. As my faith grew in God, so did my trust. I have heard over and over that He loved me and I've shared some of those times with you. Still it was hard to trust those words, even from God. I'm eternally thankful He is so patient with me. He has let me learn at my own pace, although I have to admit sometimes I felt Him pushing me to *go* somewhere I really didn't want to. God's heart is to see me healed, and He has used people, places and words. Read this journal entry I made one morning, followed by words He gave me while sitting in church. See the battle I was in. Also see His presence in it.

Lord, you're asking me to step out of my flesh, my fears,

and step into Your arms of love. You are my rescuer. You're asking me to step up into a new level with You. Lord, I'm trying, I really, really am. "I know, Child, I know. This is all new to you. Just one more step. We'll do this one step at a time. Write it, write what I'm telling you about contained life."

Here's what followed a few days later.

Lord, it struck so hard when I listened to Pastor Rusty. I felt like the walls of my container, my life, my pit started cracking wide open. I feel that life as I've known it is being drained out of me. I feel like I'm drowning in fear. I've taken off my floaties, I've stopped holding my breath, but I find myself reaching out for them and they're drifting away! Panic has set in! I'm gasping, Lord. Just like a drowning person fights against their rescuer, I'm fighting against You. And I don't want to. It seems to be a built-in, natural response of mine to survive the way I've always survived. Lord, I know I must go down. I know that You will raise me up. I know You are holding me even in the midst of all of my threshing. Lord, I know the container is cracking and that is good. I know that rivers of living water will flow and flood through me. I know this is what I really want. Then why am I battling? Fear...

My contained, pit life had burst wide open because of God's consistent messages to me. And speaking of consistency, remember when I wrote about my first few steps towards freedom...about Joshua at the end of chapter one? Well, *ten years later* this is what I journaled:

I bought Beth Moore's DVD called *A Beautiful Mind*. As I listened to her teaching *Pressing Past Our Fear*, I knew You were speaking to me. I knew that like Joshua the warrior, I, too, am a warrior. And like him, I'm standing before You seeking assurance. You told Joshua over and over again, "Be strong. Be courageous."

Lord, I almost leapt out of my chair when she started talking...ten years ago You used these same scriptures to guide and protect me in San Antonio. Here they are again at another major crisis in my life. Lord, I'm trying to be strong, but I feel naked, so unsure of myself. I find I can't even carry on conversations because I fear saying the wrong thing. I feel and know You are creating a new Carol...Lord, this is frightening. The old me is falling away and I seem only to respond in anger or silence. Neither are good.

Like Joshua, You're taking me where I've never been before. I'm moving forward with You, Lord, but I'm not a beautiful sight right now. Inside and sometimes on the outside, I'm a screaming mess! You are touching and healing the rawest parts of my being right now and it hurts. You're telling me to work out this time with fear and trembling. Lord, I *am* fearful and I *am* trembling. I'm trusting that Your arms of love are around me, trusting that You and You alone will hold me tight, regardless of how I act and feel. You love me unconditionally. Like the priests who, in faith, but trembling in fear, put their toes into the raging Jordan, I step into my river of fear. Lord, I trust You will not let me drown. You are my air…the breath of life. You are Life.

Well, I *didn't* drown, because here I am writing this story! I've learned how to swim in His love. I'm now learning to see what He wants me to see and to join Him there to do what only I can do…what He created me to do. One morning I wrote, "Lord, open my eyes to see and feel Your love's shield around me. Replace my flesh shield for Your shield. You're asking me to face my fears in order to heal. You're asking me to trust You, period. You are faithful. You will always take care of me."

God has taken care of me even when my world was being shaken. I wrote during one of these shakings:

Things will be removed. This can either break me or strengthen me. Yes, things are being removed from my life. You are shaking everything. Removing some things…yes, removing old things to replace with new. I've been given a kingdom that cannot be shaken. You cannot be shaken. I cannot be moved, because I am in You and You are in me. You want me to stretch out my weaknesses to You. You will saturate my weaknesses with Your strength. Reveal my weaknesses, Lord…please reveal them. My weaknesses are a gift.

What? My weaknesses are a gift? I've spent my entire life concealing my weaknesses. Revealing them always led to hurt…and now You want me to not only reveal them, but to offer them as a gift to You. You want to share Your strength with me in these places.

Whoa! This was a totally new way of looking at my weaknesses. It was a totally new level of trust. The questions on the table were, "Do I love You enough to trust You with my weaknesses? Do I trust Your Word enough *to believe You*, not just *believe in You?*"

This was a major step towards true trust. But trust Him I did and still do, for He has proved to be faithful. He says in 2 Corinthians 12:9, "My grace is sufficient for you, for My power is made perfect in weakness." And later in the same chapter: "For when I am weak, then I am strong."

Because you're reading this story, you are seeing His faithfulness to keep His Word. You're seeing a life of weakness, failure, despair, anger, and so much more being healed as I've presented these issues to Him one by one. Each presentation or gift has been handed to Him in utter faith and trust; trust that He will heal, repair and restore. He has never failed on that promise. I even wrote, "Anything You reveal, You will heal. I must be willing to let You look."

I have been willing to let Him reveal because I so want to be healed and to be the whole child He created me to be. And by now you know that I sit and write my thoughts and wait for Him to talk back. I write to Him in the good times and in the bad. I write to Him when I am confused, hurt, angry and unsure. I recently wrote:

God, I feel such a mixture of emotions right now. Agitation, frustration, overwhelm, weariness, and pain. What am I to do with all these emotions? Why aren't there positive emotions?

He responded, "Rest, Child. I asked you to rest. Be still. Be with me. You keep putting other things before Me. Why? Are you afraid of what I'll say? I won't harm you. I only have good things for you. Why have you stopped journaling? I've missed you."

My response was, "I'm sorry, Father, it's 6:35pm and I'm so stressed right now I can hardly think. I want to cry.

Please note that I didn't answer His question, I just made an apology. He loved me anyway. He is so very patient. He will be with you too. He's patient with my constant questions…you know, like little two or three year olds who say, "Why this? Why that? Why? Why? Why?" Well, He constantly and lovingly answers my questions as I tug on His sleeves, constantly dropping pearls of truth or wisdom into my life.

Here is what God recently dropped into my spirit while writing this book:

"Unless I receive, I can't release love to others." Wow! I want so much to release what He has given to me. I can hardly contain myself, because as I'm writing this now, He just revealed *how much love and healing He has already released in me...He JUST REVEALED IT TO ME*. I am in Chapter 5 of writing this book, having reread all of my journals, picked points from each of them, entered them into the computer, sorted them by topic, and then reread them again, and started writing. It's amazing that I'm *just now* beginning to see how much love and healing He has released in me. Call me dense.

What can I say except, 'Oh God, thank you for Your constant presence while writing this book. Thank you for teaching me and loving on me as I try to reach out and love on the reader through this gift of writing. Thank you for Your constant love and Your fervent desire for me to be healed and free. Thank you, thank you. God, let me see what You see in me and be what You created me to be. My true identity, my address is in You. Let my strength come from You. I am the right age to do what You are calling me to do and embrace what I'm good at. You're building a new capacity in me. It's my time to run in who I am, not just walk. You are my retirement. You are my Provider, my Husband, my Present, my

Future, and my Caretaker.'"

You would think after writing and reading the above that I finally *got it*. Well, I did at least partially, because here I am writing my first book at 70 years old...the right age, I guess. I wasn't real sure of that, but God was. He is building a new capacity in me. Honestly, I have no idea what that really means or entails. A book number two? Only He knows. I'm just willing to believe and trust that He has it all worked out, and that's all He expects. He will be my provider in these turbulent times because that was how He introduced Himself to me years ago. He is my Jehovah Jireh, which means God will provide. He told me it's important to stay needy, stay hungry and stay teachable. Here is one of my prayers to Him:

"Feed me, Lord, in Your presence. You have protected and fed me thus far...through trauma, storms, life-threatening trials and fearful situations. Make me more aware of Your presence in my daily moment-to-moment walk. You promise if I draw closer to You, You will draw closer to me. Give me a hunger and thirst for Your Word, Your presence. I love You, Lord. Help me to love You more.

Yes, I want to stay needy, hungry and teachable. It's my desire to learn to love Him more. After all, He is love and He loved me first. He is the expert on love. Who better to learn love from? Pouring out to others what He has poured in and continues to pour into me is now my life's work. He was preparing me to be in His presence, and His presence has been my schooling. Help me be a very good student, Lord! This is one of those times when I really want to be the teacher's pet!

Chapter 6

The Teachings Continue

"I will instruct you and teach you in the way you should go."
Psalm 32:8

Love has been the bridge that God has used to bring me out of my pit and place my feet on this mountain we are climbing; the mountain of His love. You may have seen how gently He approached me and how gently He has urged me to take one more step closer to Him. You have seen me fall, Him pick me up, and then urge me forward. The image of a baby just learning to walk comes to mind. That's exactly what I was: a baby that needed to walk in a new life – His life. I was a new baby learning how to love. Love is a part of me, because He was in me and He is Love. He is teaching me to love like He does, and because this is so radically different for me, I've asked Him to constantly remind me that's what He's doing.

God gave me the following truths. I have to admit that at the time I was receiving this, I felt totally alone with Him even though there were approximately 100 other women around me. He speaks anytime, anyplace and any way. Never confine Him to just your quiet time, your scheduled time. He doesn't do schedules. Having said all that, here's what He had me writing.

I feel like I'm in a mighty whirlwind, in the eye of the storm. You showed me it was a mighty firestorm consuming all around me, protecting me. You, Lord are that firestorm. I saw myself in a circle of life, a circle of love. You died to bring me into that circle. You reached out. You reached down, pulled me, drew me out of the pit and placed my feet on high places.

"Do you feel the hugs, the love? We are your family. We are complete. You were part of My forever plan. Welcome home, Child. Welcome home. I have been waiting for this time. I am your Source for everything. You lack nothing. Just reach for it. I'm holding it out to you. I give good and precious gifts. Drink deep. You are sealed. You are mine. Nothing can harm you. I am guarding you. I've done battle for you, now battle alongside of me. You have the weapons. Your sword is getting sharper and sharper each time you use it. Wield it in faith and in My power. I've given you the power. You know this. I know your heart. That's why I'm pressing in. I'll fill every crevice with my pure love. You must pursue…you must. The time is now."

I had to catch my breath first, then really focus on what He had said. With the focus came the question, "Do I really believe and trust His words?" *If I do, then I must step forward boldly.* Because we always have a choice when it comes to the lessons God teaches, I chose to believe and trust His words. I chose to let Him continue the work He was doing in me. I chose to seek His approval only, His encouragement and His confidence. I chose to stand in the circle and link hands with my Heavenly Father, His Son and the Holy Spirit. I chose to believe that I was encircled with His love. I chose to let Him make me lovable. I chose to let Him smooth the rough places and bring forth the new. This circle is never ending. The awareness of who I am linked up with in the circle has changed my life. I am not alone!

Please pause in reading and let those words sink deep into your spirit.

Not only am I not alone, but I am loved beyond my comprehension. He went on to tell me, "Receive my love. You aren't alone. Feel me next to you every moment of every day. I am here. You are pouring yourself out. I pour Myself into you. Continue to take Me in. Wear Me. You're getting it, Child. It's not difficult…daily, hourly in the small things. See, I'm already showing you. You are hearing. This is good. This is real. Move with Me. My yoke is light."

As I progressed in learning to walk and move in Him, I came to a new realization so freeing that I can hardly wait for everyone to experience it. Here's the new, life-changing realization I discovered: I don't have to work at pleasing people! I only need to focus on pleasing Him. Chains began falling off as this lesson became a reality in my new life. I had always been a people pleaser. That was a major key to survival and finding acceptance. If I pleased them, then I wouldn't get hurt, instead I would get praise, which meant I was significant or...are you ready...*that I was visible* and I mattered. I was a pretty sick puppy to have this belief system, but many of you reading know exactly what I'm saying. When I performed at an exceptional level, when I behaved like an overachiever, that was when I felt visible. I remember the exact moment when God caused this lesson to become a reality in my life.

One Monday morning I was volunteering at church, and one of the pastors asked me into her office. She then proceeded to ask me to take over the daily operations of the church's bookstore. After my initial shock, I explained that I had never done any retail work in my life, but that the principles of management would apply and if they were willing to trust me with the bookstore, I was willing to try. With agreement all around, I immediately set out to do *my thing*.

I went into the bookstore, looked at it with new eyes, prayed, and then began sorting and rearranging every book on every shelf. I ended up moving at least 50 percent of them twice, because the initial placement didn't seem right. After they were all rearranged, I made signs, found the coolest acrylic holders to adhere to the front of the shelves, bought some floor lights and rugs, flung open the doors on Sunday morning, and invited everybody in.

What was so special about all of that? Well, later when my pastor commented on the beautiful results, I realized that I had done all of this work to please God, not the church, not its leaders and not the people. I didn't know what I was doing, but I trusted that He did. I just followed His lead.

That was an *ah-ha* moment. *I worked to please You, God...just You.* I realized that if I have good intentions in my heart and follow God, then He makes it all turn out okay. I just need to focus on pleasing Him. The freedom this brought to me is really indescribable. It was only enhanced further when He said, "Relax, Child. You don't have anything to prove to anybody. You are sufficient as you are. You are complete. I AM all you need." He wanted me to know He was the most important thing in my life. Just putting this truth down on paper makes me gasp and catch my breath again!

I am free from working to please other people. I'm not responsible for what they think or do. I am only responsible to Him for my actions and words.

If you haven't yet experienced this freedom, oh how I pray for the day you will find this truth and start walking in it. It's amazingly freeing, and to think He used my everyday life to bring teachable moments...just like parents do with their children, God was doing with me. I just needed to be open to those moments, and stay open.

I strive to stay teachable and open to whatever He is showing me. With this in mind, I came to a screeching halt when I read something the other day out of *Hosting the Presence*, by Pastor Bill Johnson. He wrote that we are governed by one of two emotions: love or fear. Was this a teachable moment? I had to stop and ponder on that statement and found that it was true. We either act out of love or act out of fear. Because I am writing this book, I've had to go back and look at my life a lot. When I looked at it again with these new lenses in place, I saw that indeed I had been living my life in fear; fear that I'd be rejected, fear that I was insignificant, fear of insecurity, fear of loneliness, fear of failure, fear, fear, fear. It had driven all of the decisions I had made to survive! It had landed me in my customized pit.

Love pulled me from my pit. Love was healing me. Love was teaching me how to let it govern my life. Love is breaking the chains of fear that still encircle me. These chains have made climbing my mountain of transfiguration burdensome. I thought I knew what these chains were and their effect on me until I read a statement about bondage, and then I was blown away by their enormity. Here is what I read in *Think Differently, Live Differently*, by Bob Hamp. See if you don't stop in your tracks and reread it just like I did.

"Stuck...blocked...trapped...frustrated...dissatisfied.
These are the words people use to describe life when they are, indeed, stuck. What they are referring to is called

bondage. It manifests itself in two main forms: either in a deep dissatisfaction that never seems to go away, or an enslavement to destructive habits or other negative patterns of living that we can't break free from. The two are connected: these destructive habits and patterns are out of our misguided attempts to quench our dissatisfaction. <u>When someone is not at liberty to live life as they want to or when certain factors are hindering their progress, they are in bondage."</u>
(I underlined the last sentence.)

Bondage...that's a strong word that brings up negative thoughts. When I say the word, I picture chains, whips, oppression, depression, captivity. That's exactly the way I had been living. I easily recognized the golden handcuffs that held me captive years ago. However, I had not recognized all the other factors that kept me in bondage and from living in freedom. Talk about an eye-opener! Understanding this word has led me to a heightened awareness of destructive habits and patterns I still have, usually stemming from the fear that's still a part of my life.

I have to admit that fear is something I still deal with. Fears of various kinds will always lurk, but may just be at different levels than they are right now. Having said that, I also believe that God is right there giving me the strength to face them.

I don't know about you, but I'm fed up with being bullied

by fear. While journaling about fear and bondage, God reassured me. Here is what He had to say:

> "Stop fearing, Child. I have you clinched in My hand. I am the Lord your God...nothing can take you away from Me. Look back – see that I've kept you from harming yourself. See that you have been hidden. We will make this journey together. Just hold tight. Cling to me!" Lord, the tears are streaming down my face as I hear Your words. I know You are speaking the truth and that it will set me free. My flesh is in a major battle right now. Surround me, Lord. Surround me with Your holy presence. I know I need to complete this and I know it will be a battle. "I am here, Child. Your angels surround you. They will protect you...just push on."

Push on is exactly what I've been doing. I certainly don't want to fall back. My time in that pit was enough to convince me that the only way to go was upward regardless of how difficult the climb might be. At least I know this time I'm surrounded by love and a strength like I've never known. Every day I'm walking in more and more freedom and gain a greater understanding of what that means. When I heard and then reread the following verse, I was filled with hope, trust and confidence. "Where the Spirit of the Lord is there is freedom" (2 Corinthians 3:17).

Think about that: wherever you're walking right now

there is freedom. When you ask Christ in as your Savior, the Spirit of Truth comes and resides in you, and where the Spirit of the Lord is, there is freedom. Bells are ringing and the angels are cheering. The Good News is really, really good!

Chapter 7

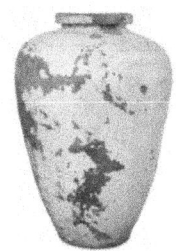

Freedom Reigns!

"Where the Spirit of the Lord is there is freedom."
2 Corinthians 3:17

Freedom reigns where the Spirit of the Lord resides. You have journeyed with me through the highlights of my life as I've learned to walk in this new freedom. You've seen and gone into my customized pit with me. You've come out of it and journeyed with me as I went up my mountain of transfiguration. You've stopped in the caves along with me and then walked out and continued up. You've read some of the life-changing lessons I've learned. I pray that as you have read, you've seen and experienced the love of our Heavenly Father, our Lord and the Holy Spirit. They have surrounded me, healed me and saved me from myself. They have saved me for others. When I learned that fact, I was once again blown away! I have been saved *for others*. Perhaps, I was saved for you.

Like me, God desires the same freedom for you; the freedom to be who He's created you to be. He understands what you're feeling and is constantly there to help (if you will let Him lead you on the journey). He knew you would read this book and identify with parts of my journey. He desires for freedom to reign in you. He desires to save you from yourself. He desires to save you for others. The Lord would say, "Claim your freedom, Child. Claim *all* of it. I have died and risen again to give it to you...it's My gift. Open it with joy. Wear the robe of pure linen, righteousness. Wear it continually with confidence."

In my endeavors to claim my freedom and wear my robe I was sometimes confused, but He was right there to gently correct me. In August 2011, I wrote: You are waiting for me to lean on You. "No, Child, you *are* leaning on Me. You are moving down the road where I'm guiding you. You will reach your freedom. You are letting Me break you. It will be painful for a while, but you will feel joy...*real* joy!"

Really? I wasn't even sure I knew the definition of joy, much less ever felt it. So, in order to feel it, I needed a definition. Here is the definition of joy according to the Webster's New World College Dictionary:

1) A very glad feeling, happiness, great pleasure, delight
2) Anything causing such feeling
3) The expression of such feeling

Okay, now I had a better understanding of the word. But was I feeling any of it?

The answer to that question was *yes*. At least I am

beginning to feel true joy. I do feel great pleasure and delight to be used by God in writing about my journey. What I journaled in 2014 also captures some of my new-found joy. It was my translation/application of Deuteronomy 32:10-17:

You found me in my wilderness, my wasteland. You lavished attention on me, guarding me as the apple of your eye. Like an eagle You hovered above me…lifted me up into the air and taught me how to fly. You are teaching me right now to fly. You will lift me to hilltops. You provide abundantly for me. Lord, thank you for lifting me up. For patience as You teach me to fly. I keep falling, but you keep catching. You will not give up on me until I am soaring! This takes my breath away and my heart beats rapidly. Lord, I so want to soar with You.

I wanted to soar like an eagle. I wanted to be lifted up by His Spirit – to see from a keener sharper viewpoint. I wanted my strength to be renewed and to run and not grow weary. I wanted to walk and not grow faint. I wanted to be Isaiah 40:31. And because this was my heart's desire, I have asked God to teach me. It was during one of those teaching moments when He told me, "Eagles go higher when in a storm…go higher, Child. Go higher."

I think it would be fair to say that I must be at a very high altitude with all of the storms I've been through. But, He was always with me, the ever present, ever patient

Teacher. He continued and continues to teach me step by step. I know I keep saying, "Step by step," but I want you to understand this and be encouraged by it. This journey you've been reading about has been taken one step at a time. Here is another moment from my journal when I was trying to take one more step.

> Lord, how I long to feel incredible deep love for You. I feel as if I am on the outside looking in. I do love You, but not like I know you deserve to be loved. Right now I feel incapable of that kind of love. There seems to be so much in the way. Is it all of the manifestations of the flesh? The real word for those manifestations is sin...let's call it what it is. Hear my cry, oh Lord. I want to experience the depth of Your love. I want to know what real love is all about. I want to love You with my whole being and whole heart. I want to live only by Your power, not mine. I want to see and feel the depth of my sin. I want to obey You out of love. Lord, I just want to be obedient, period.

> You have chiseled already on my life, cutting away the damage, but there are still so many layers of yuck that still need to come off. Where is the backside of my desert? How will I get there with all that happens on a daily basis? Please Lord, keep telling me it's alright, that we will make it together, that You will not harm me, that I can totally trust You. Yes, I can totally lean on You. In my head I

know that's all true, but I'm not sure my heart fully believes it yet. What will You do to unblock the stuff between my head and heart?

Here was His response, "Child, I have a plan for you. A plan to give you hope, a future. I will reveal it to you, if you will seek Me with all of your heart." I am trying Lord. I really am. "I know, Child, I know. It will be okay. Relax, Child. Rest. You are still so tired. Just rest in my presence. You feel it don't you?" Yes Lord, I do. "Be still. Come now, Child. One step at a time. I will lead, you follow."

God's message to me throughout has been to rest and relax. God knows us well – much better than we know ourselves. I had never learned to relax. I don't know about you, but for me to relax equaled danger and I was always trying to protect myself. Relaxing meant I wasn't doing or producing, which was the only role I was valued and accepted in, or so I thought. That's what the pit was all about. To learn to relax and rest in Him was a whole new way of thinking and acting for me. I have struggled to learn that lesson. It doesn't come naturally, but I was going to be okay. I was going to be protected. I am loved.

When our wounds are deep the healing has to be deep, and therefore we need constant assurance that He is real and we're loved. I am so very thankful for how He has used everything in my life thus far to teach me. *Nothing has been wasted*. Even the years of loneliness are being used. Where I once felt despair, I now realize I was being protected. When I wasn't a part of the *in crowd*, He was protecting me from all kinds of temptations that come with that crowd.

He had set me apart just like He did King David. And like David, I used my time alone to hone a skill. And like David, I didn't know how this skill would be used by God in the future. To me, I was just passing the time, but God knew better. David's skill was his ability to use a slingshot with deadly force and accuracy. My skill is being displayed through the writing of this book. As a young person, reading occupied my mind and taught me about my world. It taught me how some people think and act. It taught me how to put words together – how to share my thoughts and so much more. If I hadn't been so alone, I would never have consumed so many books. As I grew older, I would never have desired to delve deeply into learning about Christ.

When God revealed how my loneliness was a gift, it took me totally by surprise! With this new perspective, I've literally spent years unwrapping it. I can honestly say I am still unwrapping and seeing new revelations. Each of them have been at just the right time…His time. He's good at doing that. Here is a dream I had and it illustrates what I thought of loneliness and what God saw. Close your eyes and imagine it.

I'm on an island with water all around it. I thought I was isolated and alone. No, instead I was being protected by

You and Your living water. It flows around and upon me. Water and fire burning up and washing away all the dross until I am immersed in You. We are one. God said, "Rise up out of the water...surge up...fling your arms wide open! Let My water flow over you. You are mine. You are doing what I called you to do. Painful yes, but great."

In a later writing God told me to keep walking. I was on dry ground and He had parted the water for me. He told me to keep my focus on Him, because I was going into a new place where He was leading. He told me His water would flow to the deepest level in me. My only question was, *what level will I allow it to go?*

It was my choice. It is your choice. It's always our choice for what level of access we allow Him to have. He will never, ever do anything in us or to us that we have not given Him permission to do. Listen to His heart in a message He gave me. See what I mean...

Everything You did, You did with my glory to show me what I can do. "DO THIS, MY CHILD. Walk in the glory I've given you. The power is yours and I want you to walk in it. Use what I've given you. You are encamped around in fire and glory." You have encircled me with Your love and protection, Father. Please help my unbelief.

After all I've shared, it's sad to say I still need reassurance, I still need to be pushed, I still need to learn.

But, I'm overjoyed at His patience. I would have given up on me a long time ago, but He didn't, He wouldn't. Remember when I wrote earlier that He desired my freedom more than I did? Well, here is living proof of it:

He said, "Be a partaker of Me. I have protected you from all the worthless things of this life. Now partake of Me. You are feeling Me calling you deeper. You see my fire surrounding you. You feel my holy heat on you. I've kept you from getting truly involved in this life. Be a partaker of My life. Partake. Be clothed with Me."

As if that wasn't enough He later told me, "I'm showing you how to rise up with sword in hand. You are welding it, Child. Be more violent. Mediate on what I've done and shown you. It's important. No more idols, Child. I am jealous of you. You are mine. You are pure, strong and courageous. You already know that. You dare to tread where others fear. I need you to clear the path for others. Listen, Child. Reach for your inheritance. You are My warrior. You are well-equipped. You know this. Hear my battle cry. Scream it out from the depths of you. I need you to cry out. This isn't just for you – it's for those around you."

All of this journey was for those around me: those who are in my life now and those to come. These words from God have been my guiding light. They have been the light of hope that kept me moving forward. They have been the reason I sit here and reveal myself to you. In the rays of hope I found trust, and I'm trusting God to speak to the hearts and minds of all who read about my journey. He will speak to you in a customized way; in a way you will identify with just like He has done for me. He promises that if we seek Him with all of our heart, He will be found. I sought and I found. What I've found along the way is astonishing, only to be confounded even further when He said, "Expect the supernatural. Expect it. I am doing a new work in you. Your interiors are truly being renewed. Many will be affected by this new work."

Years ago in my broken place, I read the story in Luke about the woman and her alabaster jar of expensive oil. You may remember the story. "When a woman who led a sinful life came into the house where he was eating. She had brought an alabaster jar of perfume and as she stood behind him at his feet weeping she began to wet his feet with her tears. Then she wiped them with her hair, kissed them and poured perfume on them" (Luke 7:37-38). Her breaking of the jar and pouring it over Jesus' feet was an extravagant act of love. .

That woman and I have a lot in common. I've brought my broken sinful life to Jesus and spilled it out before Him. I pray that the fragrance of my life fills the hearts and minds of those who read this story.

And, just like He accepted the woman's gift of love, He accepted the gift of my life...my love. Knowing this woman's story holds a special meaning for me, He prompted a friend to give me a beautiful, solid alabaster box to hold my own oils. At the time she had no idea I was writing this story. She just heard Him tell her to give it to me. What an incredibly perfect gift! So unexpected, so very precious. Only He knew what her gift would mean to me. This was truly a customized gift. It symbolizes the first step I took in my journey to freedom: to live and not just exist. How do you say thank you for such a priceless gift? Words fail me, but I know the oil symbolizes pouring out whatever He pours into me.

And so here we are – me writing, you reading, Him pouring into me, and me pouring into you. Recently I wrote in one of my journals, "I'm amazed, Lord, at the things You have brought me through. I'm amazed at how You've caused me to reflect on them and begin writing the facts down. The reality is, my past experiences mixed with Your words and love have made me who I am right now."

I am still taking in the truth of those words. Had I not started journaling long ago, this story would not have taken shape. As you read about my journey, see a story of love and how love can heal the most broken person. His love has transformational power.

Anyone can take a profound journey like mine, and it all starts with one step. Your journey is as precious to Him as mine. The words spoken to me are for you, too. I've learned that each of us is special to Him. Each of us are the apple of His eye. Each of us have our name imprinted on the palm of His hand. I have learned that He, the Creator and Maker of all that we see, hear, feel, and experience sings and dances over us. I know I still have much to learn, but I've learned to run in His boundless freedom. I understand how to read His Word, listen for His voice and to apply what I hear. I want to leave you with what I heard in Psalm 132:11-18 and how I wrote my prayer back to Him. I urge you to sit in a quiet place, read His Word and listen for His voice. I promise you His full, thriving life, will not be dull in any way.

Thank you, Lord, for not only hearing my prayers, but answering them beyond measure. Thank you for dwelling in me and teaching me in the gentlest way. Thank you for keeping Your promises...all of them! You reside in me, but will come again soon and very soon, to make Your home here on the new earth. You will make it new again as You are making me new again. Words fail to express what that means to me, but You Lord, know my heart.

I went on to write, "Thank you for residing in me. Thank you for not re-arranging my thoughts, actions and attitudes, but rather renewing them. You are painting the walls of my soul and my mind with Your glory. All I do, say, think and hear will reflect You. Paint, Lord, with an impenetrable paint. Let Your Word, Your glory, Your presence be all that others see when they come in contact with me. You deserve all the honor and all the glory."

My Heavenly Father is still painting. I am still writing and listening as I continue on my journey. And yes, *freedom still reigns*!

Starting Your Own Journey with God

Some who have read the draft of this book before it was published have asked me to guide them along their own journey. My response has been the same to each of them. "This is a journey uniquely designed by God just for you." Having said that, I can give you some general guidance.

1. You must **be totally honest with yourself**, especially in the painful times.

2. At the onset of your quest, make the decision to persevere. For example, I knew the hell I had lived through and I didn't want to go back to it or continue in it. Forward was the *only* way I was going.

3. **You have to own your own healing...be determined to be honest.**

4. Healing requires time. I wish I could tell you it happens overnight, it doesn't. This is a lifetime endeavor, one step at a time.

5. There will be tears. Lots of tears. Remember that "tears bathe the soul," and wounded souls need to shed lots of tears.

6. There will be anger, maybe even rage. There will be times that you can't seem to move at all. Don't despair, He is working on the inside of you. It will come to the surface in His timing.

7. Determine to sit and read your Bible daily. It's God's love letter to you. I insert my name or say *me* in places to personalize it. When He talks about enemies, I list the ones I am fighting that day. For example it may be a situation, a co-worker I'm at odds with, my health, my finances. The list could go on and on.

8. *Listen* for His voice. Journal what you are reading, what you are feeling, what's happening. Journal what He tells you. I'd suggest starting with Psalms, after all David experienced rejection, shame, anger, joy, and depression. Who better to learn from? To help you better understand what I'm saying, I've copied two of my Psalm entries for you to see. I read the Psalm and then applied it to my life on that day.

Psalm 5: 10, 13, 16

You hear me. You hear my heart. You make sense out of my words. You delight that I have come and laid out my daily challenges to You. You and You alone invite me to come to Your banquet table and to sit and eat in Your presence! You will take care of all of the nay-sayers in my life. All whose words could devastate me. You surround me with Your favor. You will "deck me out in delight." Oh what a wonderful thing to look forward to!

Psalm 6

I can cry out to You. I can cry myself to sleep. I may not get an answer immediately, but I KNOW that You hear and that You will respond. I know you know when I am so very tired. I know You will win this battle. I know you are the Victor. I know Lord, I know. I thank You for this knowledge that will see us through the darkness. Thank you for always being faithful, even when I am not.

9. I just said journal. I used to journal in small devotional books. I then moved to standard sized spiral notebooks. My final step was to move to the computer. Whatever method you choose, journal. **Please, please journal. I can promise you that as time passes, you will forget what He has spoken to you.** Capture it quickly. What you say and what He says back to you is far, far too important to forget. I am still stunned at how much He's said to me slipped my mind until He told me to write my story and I re-read my journals.

10. I play worship music softly in the background. I very much want to be surrounded by His presence and the Bible tells me He inhabits the praises of His people.

11. Take part in Bible studies that help you to grow. Beth Moore and Priscilla Shirer have excellent studies. I took part in a group setting, but you can get them online. In either case, get the corresponding workbook and do the homework. God has taught me more than I can even begin to express during those times of study. Right now I'm working through *Hosting the Presence,*

by Bill Johnson and his teachings blow me away! I'm definitely going to another level with my Heavenly Father.

12. Above all pray. Pray before you begin your day. Pray during the day. Say the name of Jesus if you don't know what to pray. Pray, pray, pray. He enjoys hearing from you. He enjoys answering you. His heart's desire is to have an intimate relationship with you.

13. Find a church that teaches the Word. Pray that God will direct you to the right one. I promise He will. He has done it for me three times.

14. Last, but not least, read books that will help you. I have provided a short list of some I have read.

Resources

Along my journey, God placed excellent resources in my path. Here are a few that I would recommend to you.

Book Title:	Author:
Jesus Calling	Sarah Young
Shepherd Looks at the 23rd Psalm	Phillip Keller
Tired of Measuring Up	Jeff VanVonderen
Toxic Love	Malcom Smith
Normal Christian Life	Watchman Nee
Think Differently, Live Differently	Bob Hamp
Bondage Breaker	Neil Anderson
Father Hunger	Robert McGee
Birthing the Miraculous	Heidi Baker
Hosting the Presence	Bill Johnson
A Tale of Three Kings	Gene Edwards
Ultimate Intention	De Vern Fronmke
Lessons Learned from a Sheepdog	Phillip Keller

Bible Study Title:	Presenter:
Breaking Free	Beth Moore
Esther	Beth Moore
David	Beth Moore
Armor of God	Priscilla Shirer
Jonah: A life Interrupted	Priscilla Shirer
Hosting the Presence	Bill Johnson

Acknowledgements

None of this book would have been compiled or written without the expressed direction of my Heavenly Father. During this journey He became known to me as Abba Daddy. Abba Daddy is the Hebrew translation of what Jesus called God in the Lord's Prayer. It denotes an intimate, loving relationship with the Heavenly Father and indeed that is what He has become to me during this season of my life. He deserves all of the praise and glory for the transformation He has made and is making in my life. Along the way He has used so many people, and I will attempt to honor them and say thank you to each one for giving of their time and wisdom. Each has been a part of healing this broken vessel known as Carol.

The staff at Valley View Christian Church in Dallas was really the starting point for my healing. Not only did they lead me to baptism, but they also opened their doors for Bible Study Fellowship (BSF), which ministers to ladies from all around the area. In my small group and with a caring leader, I began to delve into the Bible and see truths I'd never seen before. Thank you for loving the Lord and ministering to thousands of broken souls.

When I moved to Houston, I found a new BSF and again when I moved to Sugar Land. As in Dallas, I was surrounded with women who loved the Lord and were pouring their lives out for others to know Him better. By this time I was a very, very sick puppy emotionally, and their efforts were indeed a sacrifice as they tried to pour His love into me.

To the staff of Minirith-Meyers in San Antonio, I will always be thankful for you. You hung in there with me as I cried buckets of tears and assured me our Lord bottles all of them up. Thank you for sharing your wisdom and knowledge with me. Thank you for showing me a new and greater way of thinking.

To the women's ministry of Kingsbridge Christian Church in Sugar Land, thank you for seeing God's work in me when I couldn't see it myself. Thank you for your support and prayer partnership. Thank you for trusting me to speak at your retreat when I was so freshly broken. Thank you for providing the opportunity for me to write what was to become the outline of my life 17 years later.

Thank you Brother Dennis Keene at Industry Baptist Church for allowing me to guide the Girls In Action group for two years. What fun we had as daddies played with their daughters at the Father/Daughter Banquet! I learned so much from you and the experience. Thank you for your years of service and your listening heart. Brother Keene, Holy Spirit has breathed on you in a very, very special way and you have graciously poured out what was poured in.

My eternal thanks goes to Christian City Fellowship in Sealy, Texas, for their total commitment to making disciples for our Lord. Thank you for the mentoring programs you developed, helping so many heal and learn who they are and whose they are. Thank you for developing the Cross Encounter Weekend as an opportunity for seeking disciples to be immersed into teachings of being a Partaker in His Life: to live His life instead of just existing. Thank you for the Advances, coffee breaks, and journeys you've coordinated that have taken us deeper and deeper into His life. Thank you for being the loving family I so desperately needed.

Thank you Kenny McDonald, who has seen something in me I don't yet see in myself. Also, for the encouragement and the incredible questions you've asked, causing me to think even deeper. Thank you for the words you spoke when you read the first draft of the first few chapters. Those words were, "Get comfortable with the word *success*, for it is coming your way." Those words brought tears to my eyes. How could this be? What do I do with them? I don't have answers yet, but I know Kenny will be right there with me helping me to sort out my thinking and giving me biblical illustrations to prove his point. How blessed I have been by him and his family.

How do I say thank you to Krista and Deborah of

Creative Force Press for making this book a reality? You hung in there with me as I went through the shock of editing, the joy of trying to explain what I saw the cover as and your endless prayers. The spiritual warfare was intense and you not only understood, but prayed me through it. You two are now part of my forever family.

Last, but surely not least, my thanks to my special friend, Suzanne, for all that you went through as I healed. You and Papa never left my side even when my anger consumed me and the darkness overwhelmed me. You were always there when the tears threatened to flood our home. Your encouragement and love were ever-present. You have been the epitome of what true friendship means. Thank you for the countless times you've read my story and encouraged me to write even more. Maybe those children's books will be written yet! Thank you for never giving up on me.

About the Author

Carol Hogan spent 22 years traveling the U.S. as a healthcare consultant and was recognized in the Who's Who of Women Executives. She then became Chief Operating Officer of a major HMO, and eventually started her own successful company, The Whole Solution. After a transformative encounter with Christ, she founded a ministry to the broken-hearted and abused called Heaven's Open Door.

Carol currently resides in Texas and enjoys speaking, writing and serving in her local church.

Speaking

Interested in having Carol Hogan speak for your next event, conference or gathering?

As a national speaker and someone who has organized events, I know that picking a topic to speak on can sometimes be daunting. For that reason, I have listed some suggestions for speaking topics. Feel free to contact me further to discuss the specific needs of your event and group.

- How to Recognize Your Pit
- Replacing Lies with Truth
- Discovering New Depths Within Yourself
- Seeking God's Face and Mind
- The Big "O" (Obedience)
- Learning to Trust HIM
- Hope: More than a Four-Letter Word
- What is Joy?
- Frozen
- Climb Your Mountain
- What is Fear and Why is it Here?
- Freedom: A Series of Steps
- Determine to be Free

For more information, please visit
www.CarolHogan.com

Broken and Spilled Out is proudly published by:

Creative Force Press

www.CreativeForcePress.com

Do You Have a Book in You?

www.ingramcontent.com/pod-product-compliance
Lightning Source LLC
Chambersburg PA
CBHW020940090426
42736CB00010B/1213